Red Earth / Latérite

Red Earth / Latérite

Véronique Tadjo

Translated by Peter S. Thompson

With a foreword by F. Abiola Irele and
illustrations by Véronique Tadjo

EASTERN WASHINGTON UNIVERSITY PRESS

12 11 10 09 08 07 06   1 2 3 4 5

The French text of *Latérite* was originally published in 1984 by Éditions Hatier.

Cover design by A. E. Grey
Cover art by Véronique Tadjo

Library of Congress Cataloging-in-Publication Data

Tadjo, Véronique
Uniform Title: Latérite. English
Red earth : Latérite : poems by Véronique Tadjo / translated by Peter Thompson.
Spokane, WA : Eastern Washington University Press, 2005.
p. cm.
PQ3989.2.T25L3813 2005
Dewey No.: 841/.914 22
ISBN: 1597660094 (alk. paper)
Other authors: Thompson, Peter.
14071559

∞ The paper used in this publication meets the minimum requirements
of ANSI/NISO Z39.48-1992 (Permanence of Paper).

Eastern Washington University Press
Spokane and Cheney, Washington

Contents

Foreword

It is hardly a matter of dispute that we have formed a certain conception of the African writer as essentially an embodiment of the public consciousness—as what Christopher Okigbo memorably called "a town crier," one whose voice, accompanied by the gong (in his case, substituted for by the sonorous rhythm of verse), declaims a message that is social in its import. There is of course nothing in the nature of poetry that prevents its application to social purposes—indeed, its origins in spoken language and its communicative function have often determined an immediate engagement of poetry, and of literature generally, with the collective existence. And there can be no question that our recent history imposed an especial burden upon our poetry, obliging it to serve as a testimony of our experience of domination and of the ensuing trauma of the post-colony.

But while this historical circumstance has imparted an urgency to our modern literature, it has also entailed a curtailment of the scope of poetry as an expression of life in all its variousness. It is here that the work of Véronique Tadjo—whose *Latérite*, translated into English here for the first time, announced a major new poetic voice when it appeared in French in 1985—derives its interest: in its interweaving of private sentiment with the social awareness that is an inevitable outcome of the merest contemplation of our present condition on the African continent. This counterpoint of focused individual feeling on the one hand and, on the other, the sense of larger events lends to the narrative movement of Tadjo's novel *À vol d'oiseau* (*As the Crow Flies*) and to her reportage on Rwanda in *L'ombre d'Imana: Voyages jusqu'au bout du Rwanda* (*The Shadow of Imana: Travels in the Heart of Rwanda*) the peculiar pathos that is the sign of their imaginative authority. For Tadjo, an immediate involvement in experience is the precondition for a complete grasp of the transpersonal; in other words, the realm of the affective provides the path to a wider human understanding.

Tadjo's poetry has come to derive a forceful appeal and meaning for us at this time precisely on this account, for while, as we have seen, she has not been unmindful of the catastrophes of our collective experience in their continuing and terrifying scale, she has sought to extend the range of our responses into that other realm of experience that is grasped at the deepest level of the individual consciousness, even when this experience is relayed in metaphors that bespeak a specific context and environment. It is this attention to the personal that emerges early in *Latérite*, in lines that, despite the immense resonance of the imagery, announce the intimacy of feeling that is the keynote of the volume:

AND WE'LL HAVE NO NEED
OF LIGHTNING
TO WEAVE
OUR SUNS.

These lines point us at once to the fact that Tadjo's volume is a collection of love poems, addressed in an essentially lyrical register to a soul mate with whom her voice is in constant interaction. Although this partner in the ritual of sentiment enacted by the poems is never heard, he is nonetheless brought fully alive for us in the series of eulogies that, true to the praise-poetry tradition that is part of her literary legacy, Tadjo addresses to him:

YOU ARE
THE GRAIN OF SAND
IN THE TIME-MAKING

MACHINE
YOU ARE
A POTENT DRUM
SWEEPING SAVANNAS

Tadjo's lover is fully represented in these eulogies, and it is in dialogue with him that the poet communicates to us her own experience of the world. There is thus a real sense in which she lives her own life adventure through him:

FOR SO LONG YOUR SMILE
HAS SKETCHED MY THOUGHTS
AND YOUR NIMBLE FINGERS
HAVE WOVEN MY DAYS

It is the assured sense of a shared sentiment and a common destiny to which the lines testify that enables her to define for him a vocation in which we must assume her own being is also fully invested:

YOU MUST GO
WHERE FIELDS ARE RIPE
YOU MUST
LEAVE AGAIN
ON THE PATH OF THE GODS

This injunction to a high mystical calling, inspired as it is by the poet's conviction of a profound communion between the object of her affections and the world of nature, designates her as the sustainer of his vitality, even more generally as the enabling principle of masculine achievement: "If you listen to my words / the river will run in you." Thus, when the female poet refers to herself as "sorceress," the term is to be understood in its proper African sense, that is, as the embodiment of a female potency, manifested here in fruitful association with the male principle:

YOU MUST COME BACK

. . .

AND THE GOURDS WILL BE FULL
OF MILLET AND RIPE CORN.

It is thus appropriate, and in keeping with the emotional tenor of the volume, that Tadjo's eulogies to her male partner are often imbued with a sensuous quality:

YOU'LL SEE
THE RAIN WILL FLOW
IN FINE DROPLETS
AND REFRESH
THE LOAM SCENT
THE MANGOES WILL RUN WITH
RICH JUICE

Here, the specificity of reference and the driving quality of the lines lend Tadjo's images their full evocative force, taking them well beyond what might seem a facile exoticism. Moreover, the exhilaration they communicate provides the ground base of the volume, an intensity of tone that expresses itself sometimes in elegiac terms, but always in what one might call a major key of expression.

The variety of moods and situations in the volume attests to a lively presence in the world, to a keen consciousness of the problematic nature of our existence, a consciousness that entails therefore a mode of action in the world. It is this commitment that the poet urges on her soul mate when she asks him to return from an "endless exile" in order to assume the social vocation spelled out in these lines:

COME DRINK FROM EACH MOUTH
THE CLAMOR OF YOUR PEOPLE
YOU HAVE TOO MANY HOPES

TO REAP
TOO MANY CHAINS TO BREAK.

These, then, are the directions of Tadjo's poetry. What our rapid survey of her first volume indicates is that, for her, the progression from personal experience to social vision is a direct one. The scope of these poems is thus extensive, for, intensely focused as they are on an affective bond between two souls, they also compose a comprehensive tale of life—"Life in all colors: green and unripe; bitter and bittersweet." And it is the art with which this tale is carried through that has established Véronique Tadjo as one of the most accomplished writers of her generation, a fact to which this translation bears ample witness.

F. Abiola Irele
Cambridge, Massachusetts
June 2005

Acknowledgments

The translator is grateful to Roger Williams University and to kind colleagues in the Department of Modern Languages, Philosophy, and Classics. Exceptional editors at Eastern Washington University Press, Pamela Holway, Ivar Nelson, and Chris Howell—along with distinguished scholar Abiola Irele—greatly improved the attractiveness and clarity of this book.

We are all indebted to Véronique Tadjo for her vision, and especially for her support of every adventure in the translation.

A Note on Translation

The poet wished to avoid the presence of footnotes in the translation. It might therefore be helpful to define at the outset a few terms that may be unfamiliar to the reader:

balafon	a struck instrument, similar to a xylophone
boubou	a bright, flowing dress
daba	a cultivating tool
griot	a poet and musician, whose standard repertoire includes tribal histories
the Poro	a secret society
touraco	an African bird, related to the cuckoo, with a long tail and red wing feathers
ylang-ylang	a species of tree that has especially fragrant, greenish-yellow flowers

In addition, the English "mortar" (for *mortier*) refers specifically to the mortar in which grains and roots are ground.

The English version of Tadjo's poems offered here stands on its own and can, I hope, claim its own poetic authority and tone. As a translator I always caution against constant comparisons of a translation with the original, as these tend merely to be debilitating to both texts. That said, a bilingual reader may notice that now and then the translation seems to be out on a limb. These are, most often, instances—such as "porches" for the French *arcades*—where, in response to a challenging situation, Tadjo herself suggested English solutions that work, even though they may not seem accurately to translate the French.

It is worth pointing out as well that the capital letters are Véronique Tadjo's innovation, and they have provoked much positive response. I have accordingly preserved them in the English version. One benefit that derives from the style, especially as the reader plunges deeper into the book, is that sentence boundaries to some degree vanish, producing a kind of blurring of syntax. More than would ordinarily be the case, the reader is able to make his or her own decisions about where to accelerate. And as the poems begin to flow into each other, the reader is caught up in the current and drawn into the longer narrative.

One final linguistic issue hangs over this volume, as indeed it hangs— both as a vexation and as a source of light—over Africa itself. That is the option, the desire, to write in an African language rather than a European one. The debate is far from settled. A prominent Kenyan author—Ngugi wa Thiong'o—recently stopped writing in English, and the polemic on all sides is lively.[1] Both Aimé Césaire and Léopold Sédar Senghor, even while negotiating the independence of African thought and of an African cultural vision, offered clear praise of French as a tool, a *possibility*. Césaire in a well-known interview and Senghor frequently in his writing spoke of French as the language they preferred for certain uses. They, and others of course, have stressed its clarity and its capacity for expressing abstractions. In addition, those Africans who write in non-African languages have made the obvious choice to seek a larger audience for their work.

This point is emphasized by Réda Bensmaïa, the philosopher and novelist, who speaks not only as an Algerian but also as a minority Berber; he says that his readership would be close to nonexistent if he were a Berberist or wrote in the Kabyle language. In *Experimental Nations*, Bensmaïa includes language in a broad attempt to limn the new postcolonial space, to define "nation" for what was then a newly liberated land: "If in fact something like a national trait did indeed exist, it was only as a goal yet to be attained, in constant dialectic with what remained alive and active in the past and not simply based *on* the past."[2] Even a non-African can imagine the ambivalence of these positions, yet in both Bensmaïa's theoretical work and Tadjo's poetry and fiction we sense something new in African writing, the kind of new way that Senghor felt personally and tried to promote as a *métissage culturel,* a blending of cultures. Simply put, we sense that modern Africans often write in English, French, or Portuguese without feeling that they have lost something or ceded the heart of their Africanness. Chinua Achebe is well known for giving this circumstance an even more positive reading: he feels that the betweenness, the mediating quality, of his situation—confronting both English and a national language—is itself generative of a new mental and linguistic energy. When I asked the author of *Latérite* about francophone theory and about writing in French, her answer rang consonant with her poetry, her novels, and the modern quality of her thought in general:

> *La francophonie* is a concept that is difficult to define. Can so many diverse countries really unify around one "foreign" language? Does it create links? I am not necessarily in agreement with France's politics in Africa. However, regarding the French language, I think we can say today that it has become an African language in the sense that there are generations of Africans who have been not only schooled in French but raised in French. French has been with us long enough to be part of our lives and to be able to translate our urban reality. In this sense, French, side by side with our national languages, is here to stay. It has allowed us to have access to the modern world, to communicate with it. But what is important is to let writers choose the language they want to write in, the language in which they are most comfortable, be it French or a national language.

To her words let us add that we are all—every day in the face of our own reality—awkward translators. The poet in her original language merely tries to translate gracefully.

Red Earth / Latérite

ET NOUS N'AURONS PAS BESOIN
DE FOUDRE
POUR TISSER
DES SOLEILS.

AND WE'LL HAVE NO NEED
OF LIGHTNING
TO WEAVE
OUR SUNS.

IL SEMBLAIT QUE LA VILLE ÉTAIT COUCHÉE SOUS L'AIR DU TEMPS. RIEN NE BOUGEAIT. LA CHALEUR PARALYSAIT LES HOMMES ET LES CHOSES COMME SI PLUS RIEN NE DEVAIT REPRENDRE VIE. LES CABRIS COMME FIGÉS DANS UN DERNIER MOUVEMENT SE COLLAIENT AUX MURS DES MAISONS. LA TERRE ROUGE INONDAIT LES RUES ET SE RÉPANDAIT DANS LES COURS. IL FAISAIT SI CHAUD QUE LE SOLEIL RESTAIT PLANTÉ AU BEAU MILIEU DU JOUR. LE BITUME PERFORÉ DES ROUTES PARAISSAIT DES PLAIES BÉANTES. AUCUN VÊTEMENT NE FLOTTAIT SUR LES LIGNES. L'OMBRE N'EXISTAIT PLUS. UNE VOITURE PASSAIT, PUIS UNE AUTRE. DES BRUITS DE MOTO SURGISSAIENT.

LA POUSSIÈRE S'ÉTALAIT EN FINES GOUTTELETTES D'OR ET LES NUAGES ARDENTS DÉPLAÇAIENT LEURS ENVIES. ÇÀ ET LÀ, UN BOUBOU AUX MILLE COULEURS FLAMBOYAIT ET DISPARAISSAIT. LES HOMMES SEMBLAIENT VENIR D'AILLEURS, LE REGARD FIXÉ SUR LA VILLE ÉTOUFFÉE. UN ENFANT AUX AGUETS CHERCHAIT DES MANGUES ROUGES ET SON PETIT CORPS POUSSIÉREUX SE CAMBRAIT COMME UN ARC.

IT SEEMED THAT THE TOWN LAY BENEATH THE ETHER OF TIME. NOTH-ING STIRRED. THE HEAT PARALYZED MEN AND OBJECTS AS IF NOTHING WOULD EVER AGAIN COME ALIVE. THE YOUNG GOATS AS IF FROZEN IN A FINAL ACT HUGGING THE HOUSE WALLS. THE RED EARTH FLOODED THE ROADS AND SPREAD THROUGH THE YARDS. IT WAS SO HOT THAT THE SUN LINGERED STUCK IN THE CENTER OF THE DAY. THE POCKED ASPHALT OF THE ROADS GAPED LIKE WOUNDS. NOT THE SLIGHTEST MOVEMENT ON THE CLOTHESLINES. SHADE LIVED NO MORE. A CAR PASSED, THEN ANOTHER.
THE WELLING UP OF A MOTORCYCLE.

THE DUST SPRAWLED IN FINE GOLDEN DROPLETS AND THE BURNING CLOUDS SHIFTED THEIR INTENT. HERE AND THERE, A THOUSAND-COLORED BOUBOU FLARED AND DISAPPEARED. MEN SEEMED TO COME FROM ELSE-WHERE, THEIR GAZE FIXED ON THE STIFLED TOWN.
A STEALTHY CHILD HUNTED RED MANGOES AND HIS LITTLE DUSTY BODY STRAINED LIKE A BOW.

IL AVAIT LA TÊTE RENVERSÉE ET LES YEUX BRAQUÉS SUR L'ARBRE. IL CRIAIT AUX FRUITS JUTEUX DES MOTS INAUDIBLES, ET IL GESTICULAIT ET IL LANÇAIT DES PIERRES ET L'ON VOYAIT SES PIEDS REMUER LA POUSSIÈRE.

LES VOITURES RÉGNAIENT SUR CETTE TORPEUR ET, DANS LEUR FROIDEUR HAUTAINE, ROULAIENT, SCINTILLANTES.

IL SEMBLAIT QUE TOUT ALLAIT FINIR ET QUE RIEN NE POUVAIT COMMENCER.
SOUS LE SOLEIL DE PLOMB, PLUS RIEN N'AVAIT DE SENS. IL SEMBLAIT QU'UNE ORBITE TOUTE-PUISSANTE AVAIT FIGÉ LES JEUX ET QUE PERSONNE N'AURAIT VOULU EMPÊCHER LE SILENCE.

ET POURTANT C'EST LÀ QUE L'AMOUR NAQUIT.
COMME SOUS LES ARCADES, JADIS, ELLE AVAIT GOÛTÉ LA FRAÎCHEUR. C'EST LÀ QU'IL LUI TENAIT LA MAIN, LÀ QU'ILS S'ENDORMAIENT DANS UNE MAISON QUI AVAIT CELA DE PARTICULIER QU'ELLE ÉTAIT TOUTE BLANCHE ET QUE SES HABITANTS ÉTAIENT HEUREUX. ILS CONSTRUISAIENT LE TEMPS ET SAISISSAIENT L'ESPOIR.

WITH HEAD THROWN BACK HE LEVELED HIS EYES ON THE TREE. HE HURLED SOUNDLESS WORDS AT THE BURSTING FRUIT, AND HE WAVED AND THREW STONES AND HIS FEET COULD BE SEEN SHUFFLING UP DUST.

CARS LORDED IT OVER THIS TORPOR AND, WITH THEIR HAUGHTY COOLNESS, ROLLED GLINTING BY.

IT SEEMED THAT ALL WAS GOING TO END AND THAT NOTHING COULD BEGIN.
UNDER THE LEADEN SUN, NOTHING MADE SENSE ANY MORE. IT SEEMED THAT AN ALL-POWERFUL PLANETOID HAD FROZEN ALL BETS AND THAT NO ONE DARED BREAK THE SILENCE.

AND YET IT WAS THERE THAT LOVE WAS BORN.
AS UNDER THE PORCHES, ONCE BEFORE, SHE HAD TASTED COOLNESS. THERE HE HELD HER HAND, THERE THEY SLEPT IN A HOUSE THAT STOOD OUT BECAUSE IT WAS ALL WHITE AND BECAUSE ITS INHABITANTS WERE HAPPY. THEY ASSEMBLED TIME AND SEIZED UPON HOPE.

C'EST UNE HISTOIRE SANS HISTOIRE QU'ON AURAIT PU ÉCRIRE IL Y A LONGTEMPS.

IL ÉTAIT UNE FOIS . . . SE LAISSER BERCER PAR LA MAGIE DES MOTS QUI FONT LA RONDE. ELLE RACONTE LA VIE COMME ON L'ÉTALE AU MARCHÉ DE MIDI. LA VIE DE TOUTES LES COULEURS: DES VERTES ET DES PAS MÛRES; AMÈRES ET AIGRES-DOUCES.

UN ENFANT FAIT LE GUET DEVANT UNE VOITURE.

TOUT À L'HEURE. IL AURA QUELQUES PIÈCES. IL FAIT NUIT. IL SE FAIT TARD. LE SILENCE S'ÉPAISSIT SUR LES TOITS IMMOBILES. LES RUES N'ONT PLUS RIEN À DIRE. RIEN À SE DIRE.

EN FIN DE COMPTE. C'EST L'HISTOIRE DE CET HOMME AUX MILLE POUVOIRS. DE CET HOMME QUI EXISTE EN TOI, EN MOI, EN LUI AUSSI. TROIS FOIS MON AMOUR, ET TROIS FOIS TOI-MÊME, COMME ON AURAIT PU SE RENCONTRER QUELQUE PART ENTRE LE PASSÉ ET LE PRÉSENT.

IT'S A STORY WITHOUT A HISTORY THAT MIGHT HAVE BEEN WRITTEN LONG AGO.

ONCE UPON A TIME . . . TO LET YOURSELF BE CRADLED BY THE MAGIC OF WORDS DANCING IN A CIRCLE. IT TELLS THE TALE OF LIFE THE WAY IT'S SPREAD OUT AT THE MIDDAY MARKET. LIFE IN ALL COLORS: GREEN AND UNRIPE; BITTER AND BITTERSWEET.

A CHILD IS ON WATCH NEXT TO A CAR.

SOON, HE'LL BE GIVEN A FEW COINS. NIGHTTIME. GETTING LATE. SILENCE THICKENS ON THE STILL ROOFS. THE STREETS HAVE NOTHING MORE TO SAY. NOTHING TO SAY TO EACH OTHER.

IN THE END, IT'S THE STORY OF THIS MAN GIFTED WITH A THOUSAND POWERS, THIS MAN THAT EXISTS IN YOU, IN ME, IN HIM TOO. MY LOVE TIMES THREE, AND YOU THREE TIMES OVER, JUST AS WE MIGHT HAVE MET SOMEWHERE BETWEEN THE PAST AND THE PRESENT.

SI TU ÉTAIS VENU
PLUS TÔT
JE N'AURAIS PAS RECONNU
TES MAINS D'HIBISCUS
ET TON SOURIRE EN SENSATION
LE MAÏS MÛR
ET LES RYTHMES DE BALAFON
J'AURAIS MARCHÉ
TOUT AU LONG DES ANNÉES
ET PASSANT DEVANT MOI
TON OMBRE M'AURAIT GÊNÉE.

IF YOU HAD COME
EARLIER
I WOULD NOT HAVE RECOGNIZED
YOUR HIBISCUS HANDS
YOUR SMILE AND YOUR SENSATION
CORN FULL GOLDEN
AND BALAFON RHYTHMS
I WOULD HAVE AMBLED
THROUGH THE LONG YEARS
AND PASSING BEFORE ME
YOUR SHADOW WOULD HAVE BEEN UNSETTLING.

TU ES TEL QUE
JE T'AVAIS SONGÉ
HOMME-NÉNUPHAR
SUR LE LAC DE MA DÉCOUVERTE
Ô VAINQUEUR FOUDROYANT
LES LÉTHARGIES ANCIENNES
TU ES ESPRIT DU MASQUE
CÉLÉBRANT LES INITIÉS
TU ES LA TERRE ROUGE
FERTILE DE CHANTS AMERS.

YOU ARE
AS I IMAGINED YOU
WATERLILY-MAN
ON THE LAKE OF MY DISCOVERY
O CONQUERER STRIKING DOWN
THE ANCIENT LETHARGY
YOU ARE THE SPIRIT BEHIND THE MASK
PRAISING THE INITIATES
YOU ARE THE RED EARTH
FERTILE WITH BITTER SONGS

GLISSE À MON DOIGT
L'ANNEAU DU SILENCE
QUI APPELLE LES MOTS SACRÉS
ET CONQUIERT LES BUILDINGS.
REDIS-MOI LE CHANT DE LA HERSE
ET LA PLAINTE DES HOMMES
DOCKERS
APPRENDS-MOI
VEUX-TU?
LES FUTURS COMBATTANTS.

SLIDE ON MY FINGER
THE RING OF SILENCE
THAT SUMMONS THE SACRED WORDS
AND CONQUERS HIGH-RISES.
TELL ME AGAIN THE SONG OF THE HARROW
AND THE PLAINT OF MEN
LONGSHOREMEN
TEACH ME
WILL YOU?
THE STRUGGLES TO COME.

MONTRE-LUI
LES CRIS DES DESSOUS DE LA TERRE
LES ÉTÉS ACCABLANTS
ET LES PLUIES DESTRUCTRICES
APPRENDS-LUI
À RETENIR SON SOUFFLE
À LA CADENCE
DES FEUILLES PREMIÈRES
RETIENS SA MAIN
JUSQU'AU BOUT DU CHEMIN
QU'ELLE VAINQUE ELLE-MÊME SA PEUR!

SHOW HER
THE CRIES FROM UNDER THE EARTH
THE OPPRESSIVE SUMMERS
DEVASTATING RAINS
TEACH HER
TO HOLD HER BREATH
TO THE BEAT OF THE FIRST LEAVES
HOLD ONTO HER HAND
TO THE VERY END OF THE PATH
LET HER CONQUER HER OWN FEAR!

IL FAUT ACCOUCHER
DE L'ENFANCE
CRACHER LE VENIN
QUI ROMPT TA VIOLENCE
ENLACER LE PRÉSENT
ET PARTIR SUR LES QUAIS
LA QUIÉTEUR DU FŒTUS
EST LA NUIT DE TOUT TEMPS.

YOU MUST BE DELIVERED
OF CHILDHOOD
SPIT OUT THE VENOM
THAT SAPS YOUR VIOLENCE
EMBRACE THE PRESENT
AND SET OFF ON STATION PLATFORMS
THE STILLNESS OF THE FETUS
IS THE NIGHT OF THE AGES.

DIS-LUI
LES VICTOIRES PARCOURUES
ET LES CHEMINS DE MIDI.
DIS-LUI AUSSI
LA SENTEUR DU PETIT MATIN
ET LE CŒUR À TOUT ROMPRE
IL N'EXISTE PAS
DE LUNE SANS ÉVEIL
PAS DE CHANT
SANS TOURACO.

TELL HER
THE VICTORIES TALLIED
AND THE PATHWAYS OF NOON.
TELL HER TOO
OF THE GLIMMERS OF EARLY MORNING
AND THE HEART POUNDING
THERE IS NO
MOON WITHOUT A WAKING
NO SONG
WITHOUT A TOURACO.

CHANTE-MOI
L'HISTOIRE
DE L'HOMME-LABEUR
SA SUEUR BRÛLANTE
ET LA TERRE TROP ROUGE
PARLE-MOI
DE LA FEMME AUX SEINS LOURDS
ET AU VENTRE-CALEBASSE
DANS LA FOURNAISE INTENSE
D'UNE NUIT SANS DEMAIN
ENSEIGNE-MOI
LES LIVRES FERMÉS
ET LES MAINS TENDUES
LES ESPOIRS BLOQUÉS
DANS L'OUBLI SOMBRE
D'UNE VILLE TROP FARDÉE.

SING TO ME
THE STORY
OF THE PLOWMAN
HIS SEARING SWEAT
AND THE TOO-RED EARTH
TALK TO ME
ABOUT THE WOMAN
WITH HEAVY BREASTS
AND BELLY-GOURD
IN THE INTENSE FURNACE
OF A NIGHT WITHOUT TOMORROW
TEACH ME
THE CLOSED BOOKS
AND REACHING HANDS
THE HOPES BROKEN
IN THE BLACK OBLIVION
OF A GAUDY LITTLE TOWN.

QUE POUVAIT-IL
ATTENDRE
DU SOURD CHEMINEMENT
VERS L'HORIZON
SANS FRONTIÈRE
CE GOUFFRE HALLUCINANT
CETTE ANGOISSE SANS FOSSÉ?
QUE POUVAIT-IL FAIRE
DE L'OPPRESSION DES MOTS
DU SANG À ROMPRE HALEINE?
LAMBEAUX D'UNE VIE
DE PAS À PAS
ET C'EST ENCORE UN HOMME
QUI MEURT AU BORD DE NOUS.

WHAT COULD HE
EXPECT
FROM THE DULL PLODDING
TOWARD THE BORDERLESS
HORIZON
THIS RAVING ABYSS
MOATLESS ANGUISH?
WHAT COULD HE DO
IN THE OPPRESSION OF WORDS
AND POUNDING BLOOD?
SHREDS OF A LIFE
SHORT STEPS
AND IT'S ONE MORE MAN
DYING AT OUR EDGE.

SOUVIENS-TOI
DE L'HOMME-BOSSU
DE L'HOMME-TAUDIS
DE L'HOMME-MOINS-QUE-RIEN.

REMEMBER
THE HUNCHBACK-MAN
THE HOVEL-MAN
THE LESS-THAN-NOTHING-MAN

DÉCOUVRE POUR ELLE
TES MILLE MASQUES
DU FOND DE L'ÂME
TES MOTS ABSENTS
ET TES TRISTES MÉMOIRES
DÉFAIS TON ANGOISSE
ET REGARDE-LA ENCORE
ALORS VOUS COMPRENDREZ
ENSEMBLE
LES NUITS OBSCURES
ET LES RÊVES AVORTÉS
ALORS SEULEMENT
VOUS MARCHEREZ.

UNVEIL FOR HER
THE THOUSAND MASKS
AT THE BOTTOM OF YOUR SOUL
YOUR ABSENT WORDS
AND SAD MEMORIES
UNKNOT YOUR ANGUISH
AND LOOK AGAIN AT HER
THEN YOU'LL GRASP
TOGETHER
THE DARK NIGHTS
AND ABORTED DREAMS
AND ONLY THEN
SET FORTH.

NOUS BÂTIRONS POUR LUI
DES FERMES CLAIRES
ET DES MAISONS EN DUR
NOUS OUVRIRONS LES LIVRES
ET SOIGNERONS LES PLAIES
NOUS DONNERONS UN NOM
À CHAQUE MENDIANT DU COIN
ET HABILLERONS DE BASIN
LES PLUS PETITS D'ENTRE EUX
IL FAUT SAVOIR BÂTIR
SUR LES RUINES DES CITÉS
SAVOIR TRACER
LES CHEMINS DE LIBERTÉ.

WE WILL BUILD FOR HIM
OPEN FARMS
AND BRICK HOUSES
WE WILL OPEN THE BOOKS
AND DRESS THE WOUNDS
WE'LL GIVE A NAME
TO EACH CORNER BEGGAR
AND WE'LL DRESS IN COTTON
THE SMALLEST AMONG THEM
YOU HAVE TO KNOW HOW TO BUILD
ON THE RUINS OF CITIES
KNOW HOW TO TRACE
THE PATHS OF LIBERTY.

VOUS LES FOUILLEURS DE POUBELLES
LES INFIRMES
AUX MOIGNONS CRASSEUX
LES BORGNES
LES HOMMES RAMPANTS
VOUS LES MARAUDEURS
LES GAMINS DES TAUDIS
JE VOUS SALUE.

YOU THE TRASH PICKERS
THE HOBBLED
WITH FILTHY STUMPS
THE ONE-EYED
THE CRAWLERS
YOU THE SCAVENGERS
THE SLUM URCHINS
I SALUTE YOU.

QUEL FARDEAU PORTEZ-VOUS
EN CE MONDE IMMONDE
PLUS LOURD QUE LA VILLE
QUI MEURT DE SES PLAIES?
QUELLE PUISSANCE
VOUS LIE À CETTE TERRE FRIGIDE
QUI N'ENFANTE DES JUMEAUX
QUE POUR LES SÉPARER?
QUI N'ÉLÈVE DES BUILDINGS
QUE POUR VOUS ÉCRASER
SOUS LES TONNES DE BÉTON
ET D'ASPHALTE FUMANT?

WHAT BURDEN DO YOU BEAR
IN THIS FOUL WORLD
HEAVIER THAN THE CITY
DYING OF ITS WOUNDS?
WHAT POWER
LINKS YOU TO THIS FRIGID EARTH
THAT BIRTHS TWINS
ONLY TO SEPARATE THEM?
THAT RAISES BUILDINGS
ONLY TO CRUSH YOU
UNDER TONS OF CEMENT
AND STEAMING ASPHALT?

VOUS LES MANGEURS
DE RESTES
LES SANS-LOGIS
LES SANS-ABRI
QUEL REGARD PORTEZ-VOUS
SUR L'HORIZON EN FEU?

YOU THE DEVOURERS
OF SCRAPS
THE HOMELESS
THE SHELTERLESS
WHAT GAZE DO YOU LEVEL
ON THE HORIZON IN FLAMES?

IL EST DES CRIS PUISSANTS
OÙ PERCE LA MISÈRE
ET DES FEMMES VOILÉES
OÙ SE TAISENT LES REFRAINS
IL EST AUSSI
DES POINGS FERMÉS
OÙ BATTENT
LES VIOLENCES
COMME UN HOMME ENCHAÎNÉ
À SA PROPRE SOUFFRANCE.

THERE ARE RAGING CRIES
WHERE MISERY SHOWS THROUGH
AND WOMEN ARE VEILED
LIKE THE REFRAINS
THERE ARE ALSO
CLENCHED FISTS
WHERE ASSAULTS
FLAIL
LIKE A MAN CHAINED
TO HIS OWN SUFFERING.

ENVELOPPE-MOI
DANS LA SUEUR DE TA PEAU
ET REJOINS-MOI
OÙ LES GÉNIES
FONT LA RONDE.

WRAP ME
IN THE SWEAT OF YOUR SKIN
AND JOIN ME
WHERE SPIRITS
DANCE IN A CIRCLE.

IL FAUT QUE NOUS PARTIONS
SUR LES PISTES DES VOYAGEURS
RASSEMBLE CE QUE TU CHERCHES
ET TIENS-TOI PRÊT DÉJÀ
PARTOUT OÙ NOUS IRONS
IL Y AURA DES CARAVANES.

WE HAVE TO LEAVE
ON THE PATHS OF TRAVELERS
GRAB UP WHAT YOU'RE LOOKING FOR
AND KEEP READY
WHEREVER WE GO
THERE WILL BE CARAVANS.

APPRENDS-MOI
L'AIR DES PRAIRIES BLEUES
ET SOUFFLE À MON OREILLE
TON HALEINE PRINCIÈRE
IL Y A TANT DE MOTS
SOUS LA POUSSIÈRE
TANT D'AMOURS
DANS LES TIROIRS
J'AI MAL À CROIRE
QUE LES FEUX DE BROUSSE
SONT ÉTEINTS.

TEACH ME
THE MUSIC OF BLUE PRAIRIES
AND BLOW IN MY EAR
YOUR PRINCELY BREATH
THERE ARE SO MANY WORDS
UNDER THE DUST
SO MANY LOVES
IN THE DRAWERS
I CAN'T BELIEVE
THE BRUSHFIRES
HAVE GONE OUT.

RACONTE-MOI
LA PAROLE DU GRIOT
QUI CHANTE L'AFRIQUE
DES TEMPS IMMÉMORIAUX
IL DIT
CES ROIS PATIENTS
SUR LES CIMES DU SILENCE
ET LA BEAUTÉ DES VIEUX
AUX SOURIRES FANÉS
MON PASSÉ REVENU
DU FOND DE MA MÉMOIRE
COMME UN SERPENT TOTEM
À MES CHEVILLES LIÉ
MA SOLITUDE
ET MES ESPOIRS BRISÉS
QU'APPORTERAIS-JE
À MES ENFANTS
SI J'AI PERDU LEUR ÂME?

REPEAT TO ME
WHAT THE GRIOT SAYS
WHO SINGS AFRICA
FROM TIME BEFORE TIME
HE RECOUNTS
THESE PATIENT KINGS
ON THE SUMMITS OF SILENCE
AND THE BEAUTY OF THE ELDERS
WITH FADED SMILES
MY PAST RETURNED
FROM THE DEPTHS OF MY MEMORY
LIKE A TOTEM SNAKE
COILING MY ANKLES
MY SOLITUDE
AND MY SHATTERED HOPES
WHAT MIGHT I BRING
MY CHILDREN
IF I HAVE LOST THEIR SOUL?

IL DIT
LE GRIOT À LA LANGUE PENDANTE
« VOUS IREZ PLUS LOIN ENCORE
DANS LA FORÊT BLANCHE
DES BÉTONS ENTASSÉS
ET VOUS PLEUREREZ
DANS LES QUARTIERS BOUEUX
D'UNE VILLE SANS REFUGE »
IL DIT AUSSI
LE GRIOT NOUVEAU
« REGARDEZ!
IL EST DÉJÀ DES HOMMES
QUE LES RÉVOLTES ÉTREIGNENT ».

HE SAYS
THE LONG-WINDED GRIOT
"YOU WILL GO STILL FURTHER
IN THE WHITE FOREST
OF PILED CEMENT
AND YOU WILL WEEP
IN THE MUDDY ZONES
OF A CITY WITHOUT REFUGE"
HE SAYS TOO
THE NEW GRIOT
"LOOK!
THERE ARE ALREADY MEN
EMBRACED BY REVOLT."

LES BALAFONS VENAIENT
À PEINE DE S'ARRÊTER
JE ME SENTAIS
DÉJÀ SEULE
JE NE SAVAIS PLUS
SI LE SOL ÉTAIT MOUILLÉ
OU SI LE VENT AVAIT TOURNÉ.

THE BALAFONS
HAD JUST FALLEN SILENT
I FELT
ALONE ALREADY
I NO LONGER KNEW
IF THE GROUND WAS WET
OR IF THE WIND HAD SHIFTED.

C'EST ICI QUE JE VEUX
M'ALLONGER
ET PUISER MA BEAUTÉ
C'EST À CÔTÉ DU MONT
ET SOUS CETTE TERRE ROUGE
QUE JE VEUX RETROUVER
LES SECRETS ENTERRÉS.

HERE IS WHERE
I WANT TO REST
AND FIND MY BEAUTY
BESIDE THE MOUNTAIN
AND BENEATH THIS RED EARTH
I WANT TO RECOVER
THE BURIED SECRETS.

POINT DE BALANCE
POINT DE RUPTURE
TES DOIGTS SUR MA MAIN
SUFFISENT
JE NE SAIS PAS
SI TU ES
MON AMI, MON AMOUR
OU MON FRÈRE.

TIPPING POINT
BREAKING POINT
YOUR FINGERS ON MY HAND
ARE ALL IT TAKES
I DON'T KNOW
IF YOU ARE
MY FRIEND, MY LOVER
OR MY BROTHER.

IL EST ENTRÉ
SANS FRAPPER
PAR LA PORTE DE DERRIÈRE
DANS UNE MAISON VOLÉE
NOUS IRONS
TOUT L'HIVERNAGE.

HE CAME IN
WITHOUT KNOCKING
BY THE BACK DOOR
IN A STOLEN HOUSE
WE WILL HIBERNATE.

EXALTATION
DE MON IDENTITÉ SEREINE
TU NARGUES LE CIEL
QUI M'A DONNÉ LA VIE
TU NARGUES MES ESPOIRS
ET MES REFRAINS PASSÉS
TU BOUSCULES MON VENTRE
ORGASME
AU LENDEMAIN
DE MA FRAYEUR
TU ES MON DÉSIR
SUR L'EAU VIVE.

EXALTATION
OF MY SERENE IDENTITY
YOU JEER AT THE SKY
THAT GAVE ME LIFE
YOU MOCK MY HOPES
AND MY OLD REFRAINS
WHILE BUMPING MY BELLY
ORGASM
ON THE MORROW
OF MY TERROR
YOU ARE MY DESIRE
LIKE BROOK WATER.

TU ES
LE GRAIN DE SABLE
DANS LA MACHINE
À FAIRE LE TEMPS
TU ES
TAM-TAM PUISSANT
BALAYANT LA SAVANE
ET NOUS N'AURONS PAS BESOIN
DE FOUDRE
POUR TISSER
DES SOLEILS.

YOU ARE
THE GRAIN OF SAND
IN THE TIME-MAKING
MACHINE
YOU ARE
A POTENT DRUM
SWEEPING SAVANNAS
AND WE'LL HAVE NO NEED
OF LIGHTNING
FOR WEAVING
OUR SUNS.

RAPPELLE-TOI
NOS RIRES MOISSONNÉS
DANS L'ÉTÉ DE LA VILLE
NOS MAINS OUVERTES
ET NOS ESPOIRS D'HIBISCUS
SOUVIENS-TOI
ET NE RENIE JAMAIS
LES MOMENTS SIMPLES
QUI FURENT LES NÔTRES.

RECALL
THE REAPING OF OUR LAUGHS
IN THE TOWN'S SUMMER
OUR HANDS OPEN
AND HIBISCUS HOPES
REMEMBER
AND NEVER DISOWN
THE SIMPLE MOMENTS
THAT WERE OURS.

VIENS TE RINCER
DANS MES BRAS TIÈDES
ET DANS LE TOURBILLON
DE NOS CŒURS
DÉPOSER TA SEMENCE
FAIRE L'AMOUR
AU FOND DES YEUX.

COME SOAK
IN MY WARM EMBRACE
AND IN THE WATER-WHIRL
OF OUR HEARTS
LEAVE YOUR SEED
MAKING LOVE
IN THE DEEP OF OUR EYES.

TU ES MA MUSE
QUI S'EN VA
MA MUSE QUI REVIENT
MA MUSE À DOUBLE TRANCHANT
LES FRUITS DE MON ÂME EN DÉROUTE
LE VENTRE ROND DE MA FÉCONDITÉ
MA MUSE QUI S'AMUSE
À ME JOUER DES TOURS
TU ES MA MUSE AUX TROIS SOURIRES
D'ACACIAS D'HIBISCUS
ET DE YLANG-YLANG.

YOU ARE MY MUSE
DEPARTING
MY MUSE WHO COMES BACK
MY DOUBLE-EDGED MUSE
THE FRUIT OF MY SOUL
LEFT UNCERTAIN
THE BELLY-SWELL OF MY FERTILITY
MY MUSE WHO'S AMUSED
PLAYING TRICKS ON ME
MY THREE-SMILED MUSE
OF ACACIA, HIBISCUS
AND YLANG-YLANG.

IL Y A LONGTEMPS DÉJÀ
QUE J'AIME CHANTER TES PAS
ET ÉCOUTER TON SOUFFLE
AU MILIEU DE LA NUIT
IL Y A LONGTEMPS QUE TON ODEUR
POSSÈDE TOUS MES SENS
ET QUE TA VOIX RÉSONNE
DE MILLE ÉCHOS LOINTAINS
LONGTEMPS QUE TON SOURIRE
ESQUISSE MES PENSÉES
ET QUE TES DOIGTS AGILES
TISSENT MES JOURNÉES
BIEN LONGTEMPS QUE JE SAIS
LE RYTHME DE TON POULS
ET LE VELOURS NOIR
DE TA PEAU OMBRAGÉE.

FOR A LONG TIME NOW
I'VE LOVED TO SING YOUR FOOTSTEPS
AND LISTENED TO YOUR BREATH
IN THE MIDDLE OF THE NIGHT
FOR A LONG TIME NOW YOUR SCENT
HAS INVADED ALL MY SENSES
AND YOUR VOICE SOUNDS IN ME
A THOUSAND FAR ECHOES
FOR SO LONG YOUR SMILE
HAS SKETCHED MY THOUGHTS
AND YOUR NIMBLE FINGERS
HAVE WOVEN MY DAYS
SO LONG THAT I'VE KNOWN
THE RHYTHM OF YOUR HEARTBEAT
AND THE BLACK VELVET
OF YOUR SHADOW SKIN.

IL EST MON OMBRE
MON PAS À PAS
MON REGARD FURTIF
IL EST MON PEUT-ÊTRE
MON DÉSIR NAISSANT
IL EST MA FORCE
ET MA FAIBLESSE
L'EAU QUI M'EMPORTE
ET L'EAU QUI ME NOIE
IL EST LÀ OÙ JE VOUDRAIS ALLER
DEMAIN COMME HIER.

HE IS MY SHADOW
MY STEP BY STEP
MY FURTIVE GLANCE
HE IS MY MAYBE
MY BUDDING DESIRE
HE IS MY STRENGTH
MY WEAKNESS
THE WATER THAT BEARS ME AWAY
AND THE WATER THAT DROWNS ME
HE IS THERE WHERE I'M HEADED
TOMORROW AS YESTERDAY.

TOI L'HOMME BUFFLE
TOI L'HOMME SONGE
AUX ATTACHES DE FER
TA PEAU ME SEMBLE FLEURIE
DE BOUGAINVILLÉES
TA BOUCHE UN SOLEIL ARDENT
AU SOUFFLE D'HARMATTAN
TOI L'HOMME PANTHÈRE
AU MILIEU DES HYÈNES HURLANTES
TU ES L'AMI DE MA RAISON
LA FORCE DE MA GUÉRISON
CHEMIN PRÉCIEUX
QUI ME LIE AU TEMPS ROCAILLEUX
JE RETOMBE SUR MES PIEDS
QUAND TON OMBRE N'EST PAS LOIN.

YOU THE WATER-BUFFALO-MAN
YOU THE DREAM-MAN
WITH IRON GRASP
YOUR SKIN TO ME IS BLOOMING
LIKE BOUGAINVILLEA
YOUR MOUTH A MOLTEN SUN
AND COOL HARMATTAN BREATH
YOU THE PANTHER-MAN
AMONG YAPPING HYENAS
THE ONE WHO CAN REASON WITH ME
THE FORCE OF MY HEALING
SHOWING THE PRECIOUS PATH
THAT BINDS ME TO THE ROCKS OF TIME
I LAND ON MY FEET
WHEN YOUR SHADOW IS NEAR.

AMI AUX MILLE REGARDS
HOMME BALAFON
HOMME CHASSEUR
HOMME DABA
TOUR À TOUR
GARDIEN-PRISONNIER-VOLEUR
POURQUOI FAUT-IL
QUE JE T'ABANDONNE?

FRIEND OF A THOUSAND GLANCES
BALAFON-MAN
HUNTER
DABA-MAN
AND BY TURNS
JAILER-PRISONER-THIEF
WHY IS IT
I MUST LEAVE YOU?

QUE J'ABANDONNE
L'OUVRAGE DU TISSERAND
LE KITA AUX COULEURS CHATOYANTES
QUE J'ABANDONNE
LE CHAMP DÉFRICHÉ
AUX LOURDES PROMESSES DE RÉCOLTES
ET DE GRENIERS PLEINS
QUE J'ABANDONNE LA CASE
SOUS LES PLUIES TORRENTIELLES?

THAT I MUST ABANDON
THE WEAVER'S WORK
THE KITA AND ITS GLEAMING COLORS
THAT I ABANDON
THE CLEARED LAND
WITH ITS RICH PROMISE OF HARVEST
AND FULL SILOS
THAT I ABANDON THE HUT
UNDER SUCH A DOWNPOUR?

J'AURAIS VOULU
VIVRE AVEC TOI
LES HEURES DE TES NUITS
D'INSOMNIE
BALAYER TA TRISTESSE
AVEC DES RÊVES FAITS MAIN
TE DONNER DES PROMESSES
TE DIRE DES RENDEZ-VOUS
MON AMI
À LA PAROLE GUERRIÈRE
LAISSE-MOI DÉPOSER
MES MAINS
SUR TON FRONT DÉPOUILLÉ
DE FIORITURES INUTILES.

I WOULD HAVE LIKED
TO LIVE WITH YOU
THE HOURS OF YOUR NIGHTS
OF INSOMNIA
TO SWEEP AWAY YOUR SADNESS
WITH HANDMADE DREAMS
GIVE YOU PROMISES
OFFER YOU RENDEZVOUS
MY FRIEND
OF WARRIOR WORDS
LET ME REST
MY HANDS
ON YOUR FOREHEAD STRIPPED
OF POINTLESS GRACE NOTES.

JE POSERAI MES MAINS
SUR TON FRONT OR-IVOIRE
ET SOURIRAI EN TOI
DES SOURIRES D'ENFANT
MAIS IL FAUT
QUE TU AILLES
LÀ OÙ LES CHAMPS SONT MÛRS
IL FAUT
QUE TU REPARTES
SUR LE CHEMIN DES DIEUX
CAR TU ES HOMME
À FAIRE JAILLIR LES SOURCES.

LET ME PUT MY HANDS
ON YOUR IVORY-GOLD BROW
AND SMILE FOR YOU
SMILES OF A CHILD
BUT
YOU MUST GO
WHERE FIELDS ARE RIPE
YOU MUST
LEAVE AGAIN
ON THE PATH OF THE GODS
FOR YOU ARE THE MAN
TO MAKE THE SPRINGS GUSH FORTH.

IL FAUT QUE TU REVIENNES
DE CETTE LONGUE CHEVAUCHÉE
DE CET EXIL SANS FIN
AU PLUS PROFOND DE TOI
VIENS BOIRE À CHAQUE BOUCHE
LA CLAMEUR DE TON PEUPLE
TU AS TROP D'ESPOIRS
À FÉCONDER
TROP DE CHAÎNES À ÉCLATER.

YOU MUST COME BACK
FROM THAT LONG RIDE
THAT ENDLESS EXILE
IN THE DEPTHS OF YOU
COME DRINK FROM EACH MOUTH
THE CLAMOR OF YOUR PEOPLE
YOU HAVE TOO MANY HOPES
TO REAP
TOO MANY CHAINS TO BREAK.

TU VERRAS
JE SUIS UNE SORCIÈRE
SI TU ÉCOUTES MA PAROLE
TES DENTS POUSSERONT
EN RANGÉES DOUBLES
ET TA GORGE
ROUCOULERA
DE RIRES EN CASCADE.

YOU WILL SEE
I AM A SORCERESS
IF YOU LISTEN TO MY WORDS
YOUR TEETH WILL GROW
IN DOUBLE ROWS
AND YOUR THROAT
WILL COO
LAUGHS CASCADING.

TU VERRAS
LA PLUIE COULERA
EN GOUTTELETTES FINES
ET RAFRAÎCHIRA
LA SENTEUR D'HUMUS
LES MANGUES DONNERONT
UN JUS ÉPAIS
ET LES CALEBASSES
SERONT PLEINES
DE MIL ET DE MAÏS FRAIS.

YOU WILL SEE
THE RAIN WILL FLOW
IN FINE DROPLETS
AND REFRESH
THE LOAM SCENT
THE MANGOES WILL RUN WITH
RICH JUICE
AND THE GOURDS WILL BE FULL
OF MILLET AND RIPE CORN.

TU VERRAS
JE SUIS UNE SORCIÈRE
SI TU ÉCOUTES MA PAROLE
LA RIVIÈRE COULERA EN TOI.

YOU WILL SEE
I AM A SORCERESS
IF YOU LISTEN TO MY WORDS
THE RIVER WILL RUN IN YOU.

LA PLUIE TOMBAIT SUR LA TERRE GAVÉE. L'HERBE ET LES ARBRES CRA-
CHAIENT L'EAU BOUEUSE QUI DÉVALAIT LES PENTES ET INONDAIT LE
TERRITOIRE DES HOMMES. ON MARCHAIT À CONTRECŒUR, LES PIEDS
MOUILLÉS JUSQU'AUX CHEVILLES, LES HABITS TREMPÉS. LE CIEL ÉTAIT SI
SALE QUE TOUT SEMBLAIT TERNE ET MALADE. LES JOURS N'AVAIENT PLUS
D'HEURES, LES HEURES AVAIENT PERDU LEURS MINUTES. L'ENNUI TAPISSAIT
L'ATMOSPHÈRE.

ET C'EST AINSI QUE LA TERRE BASCULA. QUE L'AIR PERDIT SON PARFUM
ET QUE LES OISEAUX NE REVINRENT PLUS. SOUDAIN, PLUS RIEN N'AVAIT
D'IMPORTANCE. UNE TRISTESSE INFINIE DESSINAIT SON SOURIRE ET ELLE
SE SENTAIT SEULE. LA CITÉ S'ÉTAIT VIDÉE DE SON SANG. PARTOUT OÙ ELLE
ALLAIT, ELLE CROYAIT S'ÊTRE PERDUE. IL LUI SEMBLAIT QUE LA SOLITUDE
L'AVAIT ENVAHIE JUSQU'AU FOND DE SES ENTRAILLES ET QU'ELLE PORTAIT
EN ELLE UN PEU DE DÉSESPOIR.

THE RAIN FELL ON THE SWOLLEN EARTH AND THE TREES SPAT MUDDY WATER THAT POURED DOWN THE SLOPES AND FLOODED THE LANDS OF MEN. EVERYONE STEPPED RELUCTANTLY, FEET SOAKED TO THE ANKLES, CLOTHES DRIPPING. THE SKY WAS SO FOUL THAT ALL SEEMED WAN AND SICK. THE DAYS HAD NO MORE HOURS. THE HOURS HAD LOST THEIR MINUTES. BOREDOM EMBROIDERED THE ATMOSPHERE.

AND THUS THE EARTH TEETERED. AND THE AIR LOST ITS SCENT AND THE BIRDS CAME BACK NO MORE. SUDDENLY, NOTHING MATTERED ANY-MORE. AN INFINITE SADNESS SKETCHED HER SMILE AND SHE BEGAN TO FEEL ALONE. THE CITY HAD DRAINED ITSELF OF BLOOD. EVERYWHERE SHE WENT, SHE FELT SHE WAS LOST. SHE FELT AS THOUGH SOLITUDE HAD INVADED, DEEP IN HER INSIDES, AND THAT SHE CARRIED IN HER A KERNEL OF DESPAIR.

MAIS ELLE SE SOUVENAIT ENCORE DE L'ÉPOQUE OÙ LE TEMPS N'AVAIT PAS D'ÂGE, DRAPÉ DANS SON BOUBOU AUX MULTIPLES COULEURS. LES JOURS S'ENROULAIENT ET FORMAIENT UN BOUQUET TOUJOURS PLUS BEAU. ET IL AURAIT FALLU QUE LE MORTIER NE PERDÎT PAS SA CADENCE, QUE LE RUISSEAU QUI COULE REMONTÂT LE COURANT JUSQU'À LA BOUCHE DU FLEUVE!
QUE LUI RESTAIT-IL À PRÉSENT DE SES MÉMOIRES ÉPARSES? UNE VASTE SOLITUDE AU CREUX DE SON SOMMEIL.

ET POURTANT, CERTAINS SOIRS À LA LUEUR DES LUNES, ELLE SAVAIT, ET SON CŒUR SE GONFLAIT DE CETTE TENDRESSE QUI FAIT LES JOURS HEUREUX. LE VENT NE DISAIT-IL PAS LA MÊME CHOSE? LE MATIN AVAIT-IL POUR AUTANT PERDU TOUTE SAVEUR ET LA MER SALÉE NE LUI DONNAIT-ELLE PAS AUTANT DE PLAISIR?

BUT SHE STILL REMEMBERED THE DAYS WHEN TIME WAS AGELESS, DRAPED IN ITS MANY-COLORED BOUBOU. THE DAYS WOUND TOGETHER AND MADE A BOUQUET EVER MORE BEAUTIFUL. IF ONLY THE MORTAR HADN'T LOST ITS POUNDING RHYTHM, AND THE FLOWING STREAM COULD CLIMB BACK UP TO ITS SOURCE!
NOW WHAT REMAINED OF HER SCATTERED MEMORIES? A VAST SOLITUDE IN THE HOLLOW OF HER SLEEP.

AND YET, SOME EVENINGS BY THE LIGHT OF MOONS, SHE KNEW, AND HER HEART SWELLED WITH THAT TENDERNESS THAT MAKES THE DAYS HAPPY. DIDN'T THE WIND CLAIM THE SAME THING? THE MORNING HADN'T LOST ITS SAVOR, AND DIDN'T THE SALT SEA STILL GIVE AS MUCH PLEASURE?

HIER ENCORE, UNE FOULE AVAIT EXPLOSÉ EN UN DÉFERLEMENT DE CRIS ET DE VIOLENCE. LA VILLE BOUGEAIT ET LES GENS N'ÉTAIENT PLUS LES MÊMES.

IL Y AURAIT DES DISPUTES HOULEUSES ET DES DÉBATS SANS FIN. DEHORS, LES HOMMES ALLAIENT ET VENAIENT. CHAQUE ÊTRE VIVAIT SON MONDE. ON PARLAIT DE MORT, DE CONJONCTURE, D'INAUGURATION, DE GUERRE, DE FAMINE, DE NOUVELLE POLITIQUE ET DE DÉMOCRATIE. LES COUPLES SE FAISAIENT ET SE DÉFAISAIENT. IL Y AVAIT DE LA JOIE, DE LA PEINE, UN PEU D'ESPOIR, UNE VRAIE RAISON DE VIVRE. CHAQUE CHOSE AVAIT SA PLACE, CHAQUE MOMENT ÉTAIT COMPTÉ.

YET AGAIN YESTERDAY, A CROWD HAD EXPLODED IN AN UNFURLING OF HOWLS AND VIOLENCE. THE CITY STIRRED AND PEOPLE WERE CHANGING.

THERE WOULD BE RAGING ARGUMENTS AND ENDLESS DEBATES. OUTSIDE, MEN CAME AND WENT. EACH LIVED IN HIS OWN WORLD. PEOPLE SPOKE OF DEATHS, ECONOMIC ADJUSTMENTS, INAUGURATIONS, WAR, FAMINE, OF A NEW KIND OF POLITICS AND DEMOCRACY. PEOPLE CAME TOGETHER AND THEN SPLIT. THERE WAS JOY, PAIN, A BIT OF HOPE, A REAL REASON TO LIVE. EVERYTHING HAD ITS PLACE, EVERY MOMENT WAS COUNTED.

PARFOIS, QUELQU'UN LA REGARDAIT, PARFOIS, DES GENS LA TOUCHAIENT. LES MENDIANTS GARDAIENT LEURS PLACES, LE MARCHÉ OFFRAIT LES MÊMES FRUITS. SAUF QUE LES PLUIES ÉTAIENT TOMBÉES PENDANT DEUX JOURS ET QUE LA VILLE ÉTAIT NOYÉE. SAUF QU'ELLE S'ÉTAIT BLESSÉE À LA MAIN ET QUE LE SANG ROUGE AVAIT TACHÉ SA ROBE DE MINUSCULES TRAÎNÉES ÉCARLATES.

C'ÉTAIT COMME SI LES NUITS SANS NOM N'AVAIENT PAS EXISTÉ, COMME SI L'ATTENTE S'ÉTAIT DISSIPÉE ET COMME SI LE SOLEIL COUCHANT N'ÉTAIT FAIT QUE D'OR ET DE POURPRE.

MAIS, MAINTENANT, LE TEMPS ÉTAIT MORT. LE CIEL SE COUVRAIT DE

FROM TIME TO TIME, SOMEONE WOULD LOOK AT HER, SOMETIMES PEOPLE TOUCHED HER.

THE BEGGARS KEPT TO THEIR SPOTS, THE MARKET OFFERED THE SAME FRUIT, EXCEPT THAT THE RAINS HAD BEEN FALLING FOR TWO DAYS AND THE TOWN WAS DROWNING. EXCEPT THAT SHE HAS CUT HER HAND AND THE BLOOD STAINS HER DRESS WITH A FINE TRACERY OF SCARLET.

IT WAS AS IF THE NAMELESS NIGHTS HAD NOT EXISTED. AS IF THE WAIT-ING HAD DISSIPATED AND THE SETTING SUN WERE MADE OF NOTHING BUT PURPLE AND GOLD.

BUT NOW, TIME WAS DEAD. THE SKY WAS COVERED IN ASH. ONE MIGHT

CENDRE. ON AURAIT DIT DES JOURS SANS PAREIL. LE VENT SOUFFLAIT UN BROUILLARD QUI VOILAIT LES HOMMES ET LA TERRE. ELLE AURAIT VOULU CRIER, MAIS ELLE AVAIT LE CŒUR EN BALLOTTAGE.

LA PEINE EXISTAIT BIEN AU FOND DE SA POITRINE COMME UN CHAT RECROQUEVILLÉ ET PRÊT À BONDIR, MAIS LA NUIT ÉTAIT JEUNE ET ELLE VOULAIT VOIR LE MATIN.

ENTRE LES QUATRE MURS VIDES DE SENS, ELLE AVAIT SENTI CETTE ABSENCE IMMENSE. LE CHAT ÉTAIT SORTI, LES FLEURS DANS LEUR POT ATTENDAIENT L'EAU DE DIEU.

HAVE SAID A NEW KIND OF DAY. THE WIND STIRRED A FOG THAT VEILED MEN AND EARTH. SHE WOULD HAVE LIKED TO SHOUT, BUT HER HEART STUMBLED.

PAIN LIVED DEEP IN HER CHEST LIKE A CAT CROUCHED READY TO SPRING, BUT THE NIGHT WAS YOUNG AND SHE WANTED TO SEE THE MORNING.

BETWEEN THE FOUR WALLS EMPTIED OF MEANING, SHE HAD SENSED THIS IMMENSE ABSENCE. THE CAT HAD GONE OUT, THE FLOWERS IN THEIR POT WAITED FOR RAIN, GOD'S WATER.

LES MEUBLES FIGÉS SEMBLAIENT TÉMOIGNER D'UNE HISTOIRE PASSÉE. TOUT SEMBLAIT L'OBSERVER ET GUETTER UN MOUVEMENT. À TRAVERS LA PORTE DE LA CHAMBRE ENTROUVERTE, ELLE VIT LE LIT DÉFAIT. LE PARFUM Y ÉTAIT RESTÉ COMME HIER LA SENTEUR DU YLANG-YLANG AVAIT ENVAHI LA COUR. ELLE SE RAPPELA CE CORPS CHAUD QUI DORMAIT À SES CÔTÉS, PAR LES NUITS FRAÎCHES, LES NUITS SIMPLES ET LES NUITS QUI DOUCEMENT S'EFFAÇAIENT.

IL PLEUVAIT. DEMAIN, ELLE IRAIT VOIR QUELQU'UN, DEMAIN, QUOI QU'IL ARRIVE, ELLE ATTENDRAIT SON RETOUR.

IL REVIENDRAIT ET ILS FERAIENT ENSEMBLE DES MONTS ET DES MERVEILLES. ELLE S'HABILLERAIT DE COULEURS CHATOYANTES ET ARRANGERAIT SES CHEVEUX À LA MODE DE CHEZ EUX. ELLE AURAIT LES YEUX BRILLANTS ET SAURAIT MONTRER SA JOIE. ELLE LUI RACONTERAIT LA VIE LOINTAINE ET LES NUITS SANS SAVEUR. ELLE DIRAIT LES LIVRES DÉJÀ LUS ET LES OUVRAGES INACHEVÉS. ELLE PARLERAIT D'UNE VOIX MONOTONE ET BASSE COMME ON CHUCHOTE ENCORE DANS LES HAUTS BOIS SACRÉS.

THE STILLED FURNITURE SEEMED TO BEAR WITNESS TO A STORY OF THE PAST. EVERYTHING SEEMED TO BE WATCHING HER AND STALKING HER MOVEMENTS. THROUGH THE OPEN DOOR OF THE BEDROOM, SHE SAW THE UNMADE BED, THE SCENT HAD STAYED THERE JUST AS YESTERDAY THE SMELL OF YLANG-YLANG HAD INVADED THE COURTYARD. SHE RECALLED THE WARM BODY THAT HAD SLEPT AT HER SIDE, THROUGH THE COOL NIGHTS, THE SIMPLE NIGHTS AND THE NIGHTS THAT NOW SOFTLY FADED.

IT WAS RAINING. TOMORROW SHE WOULD GO SEE SOMEONE, TOMOR-ROW WHATEVER HAPPENED, SHE WOULD WAIT FOR HIS RETURN.

HE WOULD COME BACK AND THEY WOULD MAKE TOGETHER MOUN-TAINS AND MARVELS. SHE WOULD DRESS IN SHIMMERING COLORS AND FIX HER HAIR IN THE LOCAL WAY. HER EYES WOULD SHINE AND SHE WOULD MAKE HER HAPPINESS GLOW. SHE WOULD TELL HIM OF A LIFE NOW FALLING BACK AND ALL THE NIGHTS WITHOUT SAVOR. SHE WOULD TELL HIM OF BOOKS ALREADY READ AND WORKS LEFT UNFINISHED. SHE WOULD SPEAK IN A LOW AND EVEN VOICE THE WAY THEY STILL WHISPER IN THE HIGH SACRED WOODS.

HIER TU M'AS DIT
QUE TU AVAIS UN FILS
   UN FILS-ROYAUME
   UN FILS-CHEVAL
   UN FILS À TOI
UN FILS QUE JE N'AURAI JAMAIS.

YESTERDAY YOU TOLD ME
YOU HAD A SON
   A KINGDOM-SON
   A MANY-HORSE-SON
   A SON OF YOUR OWN
A SON THAT I WILL NEVER HAVE.

SEXE RAIDE, TENDU
CUISSES OUVERTES À L'AMOUR
VISAGE DÉCOUVERT
DANS LA PÉNOMBRE DE LA NUIT
SES YEUX—MÉTAMORPHOSE
À PRÉSENT RIEN N'A DE SENS
RIEN N'A PLUS D'IMPORTANCE
QUE LES BATTEMENTS IRRÉGULIERS
D'UN CŒUR DE GAMINE
QUI S'AFFOLE.

SEX STIFF, JUTTING
THIGHS OPEN TO LOVE
FACE UNVEILED
IN THE PENUMBRA OF NIGHT
HIS EYES—METAMORPHOSIS
FOR NOW NOTHING HAS MEANING
NOTHING MATTERS ANYMORE
EXCEPT THE IRREGULAR BEATING
OF A YOUNG GIRL'S HEART
RACING WILD.

SOLEILS ÉTEINTS
ET PROMENADES SOLITAIRES
VERS LE MONT KORHOGO
LES OISEAUX
CHANGENT DE CAP
QUEL CHEMIN AS-TU PRIS
POUR EFFACER TES CRAINTES
ET VERS OÙ
ME CONDUISENT
LES AILES DES MIGRATEURS?

SUN BURNED OUT
AND LONELY WALKS
TOWARD MOUNT KORHOGO
THE BIRDS VEER OFF
WHAT PATH DID YOU TAKE
TO ERASE YOUR FEARS
AND WHERE
AM I LED
BY THESE MIGRATING WINGS?

FALLAIT-IL QUE TU MEURES
POUR QUE JE RENAISSE?
QUE DES CENDRES
ÉCLATE UN SOLEIL VIOLENT?
QUE NOS CRIS
NOS MURMURES
NE S'EN TIENNENT QUE LÀ?
FALLAIT-IL LE FEU
SUR LA SAVANE HERBEUSE
NOS ESPOIRS ÉVENTRÉS
À COUPS D'ANNÉES PERDUES?

DID YOU HAVE TO DIE
FOR ME TO BE REBORN?
FOR ASHES
TO BURST A BRUTE SUN?
FOR OUR CRIES
AND OUR MURMURING
TO HOLD FAST IN THAT PLACE?
MUST THERE BE FIRE
ON THE GRASSY SAVANNA
OUR HOPES GUTTED
UNDER THE STROKES OF LOST YEARS?

ÉTREINTE VENIN
LE GARROT
ME FAIT MAL
EN UNE NUIT
J'AI PERDU
LA FORCE DE MES POIGNETS.

VENOM EMBRACE
THIS GARROTE
IS HURTING ME
IN ONE NIGHT
I'VE LOST
THE STRENGTH IN MY WRISTS.

SOUS UN VOILE DE REINE
LA VIE MASQUE SES REGRETS
CES GESTES LENTS ET DOUX
CES SOURIRES BIENHEUREUX
ONT DES RELENTS DE GRANDE TRISTESSE
AH! QUELLE TRAHISON
QUE CES COINS OMBRAGÉS
EN PLEIN CŒUR DE MIDI!

UNDER A QUEENLY VEIL
LIFE MASKS ITS REGRETS
THESE GESTURES SLOW AND GENTLE
THESE HAPPY SMILES
HAVE THE MUSTINESS OF GREAT SORROW
AH! WHAT BETRAYAL
THESE SHADOWY CORNERS
IN THE HEART OF NOON!

TE SOUVIENS-TU
DE CES ANNÉES GLORIEUSES
OÙ TOUT RESTAIT À FAIRE
QUAND NOS RIRES
DE DIAMANT ROSE
CACHAIENT L'ASPECT LUGUBRE DES CHOSES
ET CES IMAGES JAUNIES
PAR TANT D'ANNÉES AUSTÈRES?
TE SOUVIENS-TU
DE CES CHAMPS EN JACHÈRE?

DO YOU REMEMBER
THOSE GLORIOUS YEARS
WHEN EVERYTHING LAY AHEAD
WHEN OUR LAUGHTER
OF PINK DIAMOND
HID THE DOLEFUL SIDE OF THINGS
AND THOSE IMAGES YELLOWED
BY SO MANY LEAN YEARS?
DO YOU REMEMBER
THOSE FALLOW FIELDS?

COMBIEN DE TEMPS
DEVRAI-JE ATTENDRE
DANS L'OMBRE
DES JOURS MOROSES
ET DES NUITS SINGULIÈRES
COMBIEN D'ÉTÉS MANQUÉS
ME FAUDRA-T-IL COMPTER
ET CROIS-TU QU'IL EXISTE
ENCORE UN BOIS SACRÉ?

HOW LONG
WILL I HAVE TO WAIT
IN THE SHADOW
OF SULLEN DAYS
AND NUMBERED NIGHTS
HOW MANY FAILED SUMMERS
WILL I HAVE TO TALLY
AND DO YOU BELIEVE
THERE STILL EXIST
SACRED WOODS?

AU FOND DE TON LIT BLANC
TU CACHES TES BRISURES
TES JOURNÉES SANS COMPTER
TES NUITS À S'ÉVEILLER
TU REVOIS LES CHEMINS PARCOURUS
LES MAINS TENDUES PUIS REJETÉES
TU LIS LES LETTRES INACHEVÉES
ET TU TE DIS
QUELQUE PART
DES HOMMES MEURENT
ET DES GEÔLIERS ABOIENT
UN VIEILLARD S'ÉTERNISE
L'ENVIE A TOUT DÉTRUIT
TU REGARDES TES BAS QUARTIERS
ET TES ENFANTS MORVEUX
ET QUELQUE CHOSE EN TOI
ÉVEILLE LA SOLITUDE.

IN THE DEPTHS OF YOUR WHITE BED
YOU HIDE YOUR FAILURES
YOUR DAYS WITHOUT NUMBER
YOUR NIGHTS AWAKE
YOU RETRACE TRAILS ONCE WALKED
WITH HANDS OUTSTRETCHED AND THEN DROPPED
YOU READ YOUR UNFINISHED LETTERS
AND YOU THINK
SOMEWHERE
MEN DIE
WHILE JAILERS HOWL
AN OLD MAN GOES ON FOREVER
ENVY HAS WRECKED IT ALL
YOU GAZE ON YOUR SLUMS
AND YOUR SNOTTY KIDS
AND SOMETHING IN YOU
WAKES LONELINESS.

HIER MON DEUIL
COMME UN FŒTUS
SÉCHÉ
DANS LE LINCEUL BLANC
DE MON LIT TOUT DÉFAIT
HIER
LA SOLITUDE SUINTANT
DES MURS ÉPAIS
FACE À FACE
OU DANS LE COMA DU MATIN
HIER
ASSISE AU COIN DES PLEURS
AU MILIEU DE LA NUIT.

YESTERDAY I MOURNED
LIKE A FETUS
DRIED UP
IN THE WHITE SHROUD
OF MY UNMADE BED
YESTERDAY
WITH SOLITUDE
OOZING FROM THICK WALLS
FACE TO FACE WITH MYSELF
OR COMATOSE IN EARLY DAY
YESTERDAY
SITTING AT THE VERGE OF TEARS
IN THE MIDDLE OF THE NIGHT.

LA VIE EST FAITE
DE RONCES ET D'ÉPINES NOIRES
JE L'AURAIS VOULUE
PLUS MÛRE ET MOINS AMÈRE
MAIS TU SAIS
LA LIMITE DES CHOSES
RECULE À CHAQUE INSTANT
LES VISAGES SE CHANGENT
ET LES AMOURS S'ÉCRASENT
LES UNS CONTRE LES AUTRES
TU LE SAIS BIEN
AU SOIR DE TA FRAYEUR
IL NE RESTE QUE TOI.

LIFE IS MADE
OF BRAMBLES AND BLACK THORNS
I WOULD HAVE PREFERRED IT
RIPER AND LESS BITTER
BUT YOU KNOW
THAT THE EXTENT OF THINGS
PULLS BACK EVERY SECOND
FACES CHANGE AND LOVES CRUSH
AGAINST EACH OTHER
AND WELL YOU KNOW
IN THE EVENING OF YOUR TERROR
THERE WILL REMAIN ONLY YOU.

RECONNAIS-TU
TA BLESSURE
ET LE POIDS DE TON CORPS
BALANÇANT SES ÉPAULES?
TE SOUVIENS-TU
DE CE PAYS IMMENSE
BAIGNÉ DE SILENCE
TE SOUVIENS-TU
DE LA SAVANE HERBEUSE
DU CHANT DES BALAFONS
DE CES NUITS MAGNIFIQUES
OÙ NOS CORPS JOUAIENT
DE LA MÊME MUSIQUE?

DO YOU RECOGNIZE
YOUR WOUND
AND THE WEIGHT OF YOUR BODY
SWINGING ITS SHOULDERS?
DO YOU REMEMBER
THIS IMMENSE COUNTRY
BATHED IN SILENCE
DO YOU REMEMBER
THE LUSH SAVANNA
BALAFON SONG
THOSE MAGNIFICENT NIGHTS
WHEN OUR BODIES PLAYED
TO THE SAME MUSIC?

IL FAUT SE SÉPARER
FERME LA PORTE
ET VA
SUR LA GRANDE ROUTE
TA MÈRE À LA FENÊTRE
TE REGARDE PARTIR
CAR IL TE FAUT ENFANTER

YOU HAVE TO SEPARATE
CLOSE THE DOOR
AND GO
ON THE WIDE ROAD
YOUR MOTHER IN THE WINDOW
WATCHES YOU LEAVE
BECAUSE YOU MUST GIVE BIRTH

IL TE FAUDRA
REGRETTER LES ANNÉES D'ABONDANCE
LES RIRES SANS RANCUNE
LES APRÈS-MIDI SANS REGRET
IL FAUT VIVRE
TA VIE DE MILLE FACETTES
DE CANARIS CASSÉS
ET DE LAIT RENVERSÉ.

YOU WILL HAVE TO
MISS THE YEARS OF ABUNDANCE
THE LAUGHS WITHOUT MALICE
THE AFTERNOONS WITHOUT REGRET
YOU MUST LIVE
YOUR LIFE OF A THOUSAND FACETS
OF CLAY POTS SHATTERED
AND MILK SPILLED.

LA VIE N'EST PAS FAITE
D'HIBISCUS ET DE ROSÉE
ELLE A LA SAVEUR
AIGRE-DOUCE
DES FRUITS DE LA PASSION.

LIFE IS NOT MADE
OF HIBISCUS AND DEW
IT HAS THE TASTE
BITTERSWEET
OF PASSION FRUIT.

IL TE FAUDRA RÊVER
DES CAUCHEMARS AMERS
ET ATTENDRE L'OUBLI
DES ESPOIRS VAINCUS
ADMETTRE TA DÉFAITE
DU FOND DE TON SOMMEIL
ET BÊCHER POUR LONGTEMPS
LE SOL ARIDE
DES TERRES DÉSERTIQUES.

YOU'LL HAVE TO DREAM
BITTER NIGHTMARES
AND WAIT ON THE FADING
OF VANQUISHED HOPES
ADMIT YOUR DEFEAT
FROM THE DEPTHS OF YOUR SLEEP
AND SPADE FOR MANY DAYS
THE DRY SOIL
OF DESERT LANDS.

IL TE FAUDRA TUER
POUR PROUVER QUE TU AIMES
ET DÉTRUIRE DE TES MAINS
LES ANNÉES DE PATIENCE
ÉTOUFFER TA FAIBLESSE
JUSQU'AU BOUT DE TA PEUR
ET SUPPORTER ENCORE
LE REGARD FIGÉ
D'UNE ÂME QUI S'ÉVAPORE.

YOU'LL HAVE TO KILL
TO PROVE YOU LOVE
AND DESTROY WITH YOUR HANDS
THE YEARS OF PATIENCE
SMOTHER YOUR WEAKNESS
TO THE VERY END OF YOUR FEAR
AND STILL BEAR
THE FIXED GAZE
OF A SOUL MELTING AWAY.

ET IL AURAIT FALLU
NE PAS SAVOIR
NE PAS COMPRENDRE
L'APPEL PUISSANT
DE SA VOIX
LE LONG RENONCEMENT
DES DÉSIRS ENFOUIS
GARDER INTACTS
LES MOTS INACHEVÉS
ET SOUFFLER LA POUSSIÈRE
IL AURAIT MIEUX VALU
RESTER DANS LA PÉNOMBRE
JUSQU'AU LEVER DU JOUR.

YOU SHOULD NOT
HAVE RECKONED
NOT HAVE UNDERSTOOD
THE POWERFUL CALL
OF HIS VOICE
THE LONG RENOUNCING
OF BURIED DESIRES
TO KEEP INTACT
THE HALF-FORMED WORDS
AND BLOW OFF THE DUST
IT WOULD HAVE BEEN BETTER
TO STAY IN THE HALF-LIGHT
UNTIL DAYBREAK.

IL FAUDRA
CONTINUER À PARCOURIR LES PISTES
ET LES CHEMINS SANS FIN
APPRENDRE À NOUVEAU
LE CHANT D'UN CALAO
NE PLUS CHERCHER EN VAIN
QUELQUES BRAS QUI SE TENDENT
OU REGARDER SANS CESSE
L'OMBRE DE NOS PAS
TU AURAS POUR T'AIDER
LE TAM-TAM PARLEUR
ET LA BEAUTÉ DES CHAMPS
GORGÉS DE SOLEIL ET DE PLUIE.

YOU'LL HAVE TO
KEEP ON TRAVELING THE PATHS
AND ROADS WITHOUT END
LEARN ALL OVER AGAIN
THE CALAO BIRD'S SONG
NO LONGER SEEK IN VAIN
A HELPING HAND
OR ENDLESSLY GAZE
AT THE SHADOW OF OUR STEPS
YOU WILL HAVE AS HELPER
THE TALKING DRUM
AND THE BEAUTY OF THE FIELDS
GORGED WITH SUN AND RAIN.

ÉCRASER TA SOLITUDE
DU FOND DE TA RETRAITE
ET PIÉTINER LES MOTS
SACRILÈGES ET PARJURES.

TO CRUSH YOUR LONELINESS
FROM DEEP IN YOUR RETREAT
AND TRAMPLE THE WORDS
PERJURY AND SACRILEGE.

SAURAS-TU MAINTENANT
RENONCER AUX RANCŒURS
À L'AMERTUME
DES JOURS SOMNOLENTS ET MOROSES
SAURAS-TU REFUSER
LES DERNIERS CHAMPS STÉRILES?

CAN YOU NOW
RENOUNCE THE RANCOR
THE BITTERNESS
OF MOROSE AND DROWSY DAYS
WILL YOU BE ABLE TO REFUSE
THE LAST BARREN FIELDS?

TU SAIS QUE TOUT PASSE
LA SÉCHERESSE PUISSANTE
ET LES HERBES JAUNIES
LES CARCASSES ÉVENTRÉES
POURRIES DE MILLE INSECTES
TU N'AURAS PLUS EN TÊTE
QUE LE BRUIT DES FONTAINES
ET L'EAU CLAIRE DU SILENCE
BIENTÔT
TU N'AURAS PLUS AU CŒUR
QU'UN BOUT DE TERRE CALCINÉE

YOU KNOW THAT ALL WILL PASS
THE MIGHTY DROUGHT
AND THE WITHERED GRASS
THE GUTTED CARCASSES
SWARMING WITH INSECTS
YOUR HEAD WILL RING
ONLY WITH FOUNTAINS
AND THE CLEAR WATER OF SILENCE
SOON
YOUR HEART WILL HOLD
ONLY A LUMP OF BURNT SOIL

DANS LA NUIT NOIRE DÉSERTE,
SORCIERS OCCULTES
ET SACRIFICES RITUELS
LES DIEUX SONT LÀ
À GUETTER L'INCONNU.
QUE FAIS-TU SOUS LA LUNE
À DÉCHIFFRER LE SABLE?
NE SAIS-TU PAS
QU'AKISSI EST MORTE
EN PORTANT SON ENFANT?

IN THE WILD BLACK NIGHT
SORCERERS OF THE OCCULT
AND RITUAL SACRIFICES
THE GODS ARE THERE
LYING IN WAIT FOR THE UNKNOWN
WHAT ARE YOU DOING IN THE MOONLIGHT
PORING OVER SAND?
DON'T YOU KNOW
THAT AKISSI DIED
BEARING HER CHILD?

J'AI CRU VOIR
LA MORT DANS LE MORTIER
ET LES ENFANTS SONT AUX AGUETS
J'AI PEUR
J'AI PEUR PARTOUT
DE LA NUIT NOIRE PROFONDE
QUI RÈGNE SUR MA VIE.

I THOUGHT I SAW
DEATH IN THE MORTAR
AND THE CHILDREN ARE ON THE LOOKOUT
I'M AFRAID
I'M AFRAID EVERYWHERE
OF THE DEEP BLACK NIGHT
THAT REIGNS OVER MY LIFE.

MAIS
QUAND PAS À PAS
TON ESPRIT SE DÉROBE
ET TU TOUCHES
DES DOIGTS
UN PELAGE SI DOUX
QUAND LE SOIR QUI TOMBE
TE FAIT PENSER AUX AUTRES
TU TE DIS
TU DIRAS
IL Y A LONGTEMPS DÉJÀ
QUE J'ATTENDAIS LA MORT.

YET
WHEN STEP BY STEP
YOUR SPIRIT STEALS AWAY
WHEN YOU TOUCH
WITH YOUR FINGERS
FUR SO SOFT
WHEN THE EVENING FALLING
MAKES YOU THINK OF OTHERS
YOU TELL YOURSELF
YOU WILL SAY
FOR A LONG TIME ALREADY
I'VE BEEN WAITING FOR DEATH.

DAUPHINS ÉCLAIRS
SUR LE CRISTAL
DE LA MER HORIZON
DAUPHINS DU FOND
DE L'ÂME
DAUPHINS DE L'INSONDABLE
ÉTÉ
VOUS SURGISSEZ DÉJÀ
PUISQUE JE N'AI
PLUS PEUR.

LIGHTNING DOLPHINS
ON THE CRYSTAL
OF SEA HORIZON
DOLPHINS FROM THE DEPTH
OF THE SOUL
DOLPHINS FROM THE UNFATHOMABLE
SUMMER
YOU LEAP NOW
I'M NO LONGER
AFRAID.

JE PENSE À SA MORT
QUI ENGENDRA
L'ABÎME PROFOND
DE TON DÉSIR
JE SAIS DEMAIN
ET LES JOURS ANTÉRIEURS
SA MORT GORGÉE
DE SANG ET D'IMMONDICES
JE SONGE À TA PRÉSENCE
PERDUE À MON ÉPAULE
LE SOUVENIR FRAPPANT
LES PORTES DE L'EFFROI.

I THINK OF HER DEATH
BRINGING FORTH
THE DEEP GULF
OF YOUR DESIRE
I RECKON TOMORROW
LIKE ALL THE DAYS BEFORE
VISIONS OF HER DEATH GORGED
WITH BLOOD AND FILTH
I DREAM OF YOUR PRESENCE
HOVERING AT MY SHOULDER
THE MEMORY KNOCKING
AT THE DOORS OF DREAD.

JE PENSE SOUVENT À TOI
JE SONGE À NOTRE MORT.

I THINK OF YOU OFTEN
I THINK OF OUR DEATH.

LE GUERRIER
SAURA-T-IL RECONQUÉRIR
LES CHAMPS BRÛLÉS
ET LA TERRE DÉVASTÉE
SAURA-T-IL
VAINCRE SA PEUR
SES CAUCHEMARS DE SANG
FUMANT DE LA BATAILLE
LE GUERRIER
À L'ARMURE SCINTILLANTE
SAURA-T-IL SEMER
LES GRAINS À LA VOLÉE?

THE WARRIOR
WILL HE BE ABLE TO RECONQUER
THE BURNED-OVER FIELDS
AND THE LAND LAID WASTE
WILL HE BE ABLE
TO CONQUER HIS FEAR
HIS NIGHTMARES OF BLOOD
STEAMING FROM BATTLE
THE WARRIOR
AND HIS GLINTING ARMOR
WILL HE KNOW HOW TO CAST SEED
ON THE WIND?

J'AI SENTI
LE DÉSESPOIR
CHANGER DE CAP
ET L'ENVIE RESSURGIR
COMME UN PLONGEON
IMMENSE
DANS LA MER TOURMENTÉE
J'AI SENTI
LE SOLEIL
RAMENER MA TENDRESSE
ET SOUS LA FRAÎCHEUR DES ARCADES
J'AI REVU LA MAISON
OÙ JE SUIS NÉE.

I HAVE FELT
DESPAIR
CHANGE ITS HEADING
AND LONGING RESURFACE
LIKE A TREMENDOUS
DIVE
IN THE HEAVING SEA
I HAVE FELT
THE SUN
LEAD BACK MY TENDERNESS
AND IN THE COOL UNDER THE PORCHES
I'VE SEEN THE HOUSE
WHERE I WAS BORN.

IL EST PARTOUT
OÙ TU TE TROUVES
À L'ENDROIT OÙ TU T'ÉTAIS CACHÉ
SOLEIL INVIOLÉ
DE LA FORCE BRÛLANTE
IL EST ESPOIR DEBOUT
AUX FRONTIÈRES ÉTERNELLES.

IT IS EVERYWHERE
THAT YOU FIND YOURSELF
ON THE SPOT WHERE YOU'VE HIDDEN
SUN INVIOLATE
BURNING STRENGTH
ON A TIMELESS FRONTIER.

PARTOUT
OÙ SE CACHAIT LE TEMPS
PARTOUT
OÙ SE LISAIENT
LES PAROLES D'HIER
OÙ LES GESTES GARDAIENT
LEURS MOUVEMENTS ÉPHÉMÈRES
PARTOUT OÙ LES MOTS CHUCHOTÉS
GARDAIENT QUELQUE PARFUM.

EVERYWHERE
TIME USED TO HIDE
EVERYWHERE
YESTERDAY'S WORDS
WERE READ
WHERE GESTURES HELD
THEIR FLEETING MOVEMENTS
EVERYWHERE THE WHISPERED WORDS
KEPT SOME OF THEIR SCENT.

LÀ-BAS, LES HOMMES
VIVENT DE MILLE SECRETS
ET L'HALEINE DES SAVANES
SOUFFLE LE LONG CHEMINEMENT
DES PISTES ENTRELACÉES
LE GRIS DU CIEL EST BLEU
ET LA FLÛTE QU'ON ENTEND
VIENT TOUT DROIT
DU PORO.

THERE, MEN
LIVE OFF A THOUSAND SECRETS
AND THE BREATH OF SAVANNAS WHISPERS
THE LONG SLOGGING
OF INTERWOVEN PATHS
THE GRAY OF THE SKY IS BLUE
AND THE FLUTE WE HEAR
COMES STRAIGHT FROM
THE PORO.

VA AU-DEVANT DU TEMPS
ET FAIS-LUI TES ADIEUX
SI TU VEUX CONNAÎTRE
TON ÂME
IL FAUT T'ALLIER
AUX DIEUX.

HEAD OUT TO MEET TIME
AND BID IT FAREWELL
IF YOU WANT TO KNOW
YOUR SOUL
JOIN FORCES
WITH THE GODS.

Epilogue

Red Earth and Modern Africa

Véronique Tadjo's importance—as poet, novelist, journalist, illustrator—invites a critical overture regarding her past and Africa's: questions about tradition and context. The line that brings her to *Latérite* (1984) and to the present is, she would say, straight—but straight like the story line in her novel *À vol d'oiseau* (*As the Crow Flies*).[1] It is a line that appears to hop-scotch as it traverses many different fields. More trajectory than tradition, it leaves us to some extent guessing about where this prolific contemporary writer will end up. And, knowing this direction even less than we do with most writers, we must proceed with extra care in discerning the signposts of her history, relying, as far as possible, on her own words.

Tadjo is a citizen of the world: she has lived in Ivory Coast, Kenya, Nigeria, France, Britain, the United States, and South Africa. Our peculiar debt to her lies in the fact that she doesn't just describe Africa; she describes the world through an African prism. This is to say that if we tried to align her with an African tradition, both "African" and "tradition" would be misleading. These are some of the dimensions (mostly contemporary) in which she thinks and writes: the modern city, life *en brousse* ("in the bush"), European cities, ancestral myth, the era of neocolonial despondency, the plurilingual societies of West Africa, the educated class in Africa, rootlessness and migration, and the life of street people. Let us begin, then, by looking at some of the lines of fracture in Tadjo's Africa.

The attempt to say for whom an African writer speaks, with whom she walks, is undermined by myriad "isms" and conflicts, most of which have arisen over the past fifty years. There are conflicts among all these groups: those not born in Africa, those no longer living there, those Africanists who have never been to Africa, those who write in non-African as opposed to "national" languages, and—sometimes acutely in the male-dominated world of publishing—those who are men and those who are women. The following oppositions are often salient: Arabs versus non-Arabs, Marxists and African socialists versus non-Marxists, Christians versus Muslims, English-speakers versus French-speakers, pan-Africanists and pan-Negrists versus anti-Negritudinists, and universalists versus many of these groups and opposed as well to the tendency to draw these lines of division so clearly. One might add to this list writers from roughly the 1970s onward as opposed to those of the first two generations. For some among these many voices, the first of all these great lines of divide was the Negritude movement.[2]

The Negritude movement grew from the friendship of the Senegalese Léopold Sédar Senghor and Aimé Césaire, born in Martinique, as students in Paris during the 1930s. It grew, too, from the status of these writers as colonial subjects. And its growth took place in the medium of the French language, the tool they adopted to promote a new consciousness of African beliefs, traditions, and talents. Although conceived primarily as a literary movement, Negritude soon broadened to encompass art, culture, and politics. As political leaders, Césaire guided Martinique toward its decision in 1946 to remain part of France, while Senghor guided Senegal to its independence, in 1960. As early as the 1940s, Negritude was a big tent and had come to dominate francophone African culture. The movement included politicians struggling against colonialists as well as artists trying to create (or to resuscitate) an authentic African voice. From Césaire's *Cahier d'un retour au pays natal* (1939) onward,[3] African and Caribbean writing radiated a new mix of pride, anger, frustration, verbal experimentation, and local color, through which the primacy of African values found expression.

Senghor wrote most of the movement's polemic and, at least up to the publication of *Ce que je crois,* in 1988, was still modifying the philosophy. This meant, most often, shading his own notion of "Africanness" (*Africanité*) in an effort to lessen the kind of essentialism his definitions of Negritude typically implied—an essentialism that increasingly bothered postindependence Africans. In the best-known of these definitions, Senghor calls Negritude "the aggregate of the values of civilization of the black world." Césaire has it thus: "Negritude is the simple recognition of the fact of being black, and the acceptance of this fact, of our destiny as blacks, of our history and our culture." These statements, like Senghor's core definitions, leave room for interpretation and even for conflict. Césaire, for one, became more and more reticent about the movement itself as the century passed its midpoint. And by the 1970s many writers had begun to feel that the philosophy had outlived its usefulness. Indeed, as a mainly francophone creation, the Negritude movement had always alienated some. The anglophone Wole Soyinka famously derided the outspoken pride at its heart, saying that a tiger does not need to go about proclaiming its "tigritude." Still, Negritude had nurtured two generations of writers who created an African ambience, African voices, and African-centered stories and poems. For an American audience, the power of this is best appreciated by considering the impact of the Harlem renaissance during the 1920s and 1930s, and likewise the awareness of "roots" and the "black is beautiful" pride of the 1960s and 1970s, and then adding an overlay of colonial domination.

Véronique Tadjo, who is many things other than a "Negritude writer," nonetheless emerges from this tradition, and she accords it its proper weight. As she explained to me in 2004, in an interview conducted in English:

> I see myself as an heir to the Negritude movement. Although I am a writer of the postindependence period, I find a lot of relevance in it. I am still moved by the poems. Moreover, when I see the state of the African continent today, with all the many conflicts that are wreaking havoc and the identity crisis rocking the youth, I feel that we still need to do a lot of thinking. The Negritude movement intellectually articulated the fight for independence.

We can benefit from this experience in the sense that today we desperately need to rally around an idea that will revive us. Sure, the issues are different. It is no more a question of decolonization, although one can talk today of neocolonization or even of recolonization. My point is that, as an African writer, I am looking for continuation. I want to carry some baggage, to have a tradition. Each generation cannot erase what the previous has done just because it is "outdated." We need to build on what has happened before, not suffer from amnesia.

We presently enjoy a modern, eclectic, liberated, and worldly moment in African literature. Véronique Tadjo is of this moment more than of specific traditions. While respectful of Negritude, she is of a generation that frequently dismisses it. And it is important to identify her generation, since the waves of twentieth-century African literature have been very distinct. Biyi Bandele-Thomas, speaking at a November 1991 writers' festival at Brown University, gave a concise summary of four generations of writers. The first is that of the "explorers"—Césaire, Senghor, Cheik Hamidou Kane, Camara Laye, Birago Diop, and others writing in French, together with Gladys Caseley Hayford, Denis Osadebay, R. J. Armattoe, and others who wrote in English. The francophone writers of this generation were generally in sympathy with Negritude. Abiola Irele has argued that even among the anglophone writers "there is the same element of racial feeling and the same compulsion to the glorification of the African past and of things African."[4] The different perspective of those in English colonies has been widely mentioned, and it is also possible that anglophone writers felt overshadowed by the prominence in Europe of Senghor and Césaire, as well as by the *succès de scandale* of René Maran's earlier *Batouala,* which, despite its candid criticism of French colonial policy, was awarded the prestigious Prix Goncourt in 1921. Still, as Irele notes, there was a common idealism in this period that presaged independence from Europe: "Realism was clearly impossible, for it was on the innocence of Africa that it was important to insist."[5] Realism, meaning a depiction of independent Africa with all its problems, came with the next generation, which includes

Kofi Awoonor, J. P. Clark, and Chinua Achebe, in addition to Soyinka. This group has portrayed itself as more forward looking and less afraid to appear Westernized. Soyinka, particularly, as both a writer of prose and a playwright, has been able to add humor and drama to his realism and to convey an existential sense of Africa in transition, rather than cherish an essential African past as a counterpoint to Europe. Commenting in 1976 on the essentialist perspective, he wrote: "Today, this goes beyond the standard anti-colonial purge of learning and education and embraces the apprehension of a culture whose reference points are taken from within the culture itself."[6]

The 1970s produced a generation, according to Bandele-Thomas, that was eclipsed by the earlier great Nigerians, such as Achebe and Soyinka—rudderless, without individual success, and profoundly affected by the promise and collapse of the oil boom in Nigeria. The realism of this group reflected their disappointment with the progress of independence and their increasing awareness of neocolonialism. Anti-Western feeling grew, along with the sense of entrapment in the industrialized world's system of banking, trade, and commodities markets. At the same time, when many in this third group spoke about Negritude, they reacted harshly to what they saw as its race consciousness. So have some writers of the new "fourth generation," to which Tadjo belongs—although she is distinct from many of her contemporaries in this regard. Those of Tadjo's generation—which includes Khadi Fall (Senegal), Tsitsi Dangarembga (Zimbabwe), Mbulelo Mzamane (South Africa), and Calixthe Beyala (Cameroon), all of whom hold distinct views on the issue—have often been intolerant of the racial and biological elements of any African essentialism. In the words of Kenya's Ngugi wa Thiong'o, "African youth is luckily composed of those blacks broken free, who are excommunicated by Senghor because they refuse to rid themselves of ideas thought by yellows and whites."[7] Some of these modern writers feel that the tenets of an earlier Africa-centered literature put a ceiling on the potential of blacks. While Tadjo has disagreed publicly with the opinions expressed by many of her contemporaries, she does belong to a generation more likely to see itself as connected to the world at large, one in which women have fared better than before in the publishing universe and one in which tempers have flared over the issue of using "the colonizer's language."[8]

Thinking of images in *Latérite*, but also looking back at these generations, I asked the poet whether links existed in her work to the past (to preindependence, to precolonization, to premodern times) or to the *parole du griot,* the language of the village wiseman or storyteller. "I am not much into all these categorizations," she replied. "When I write, I am not aware of all of them, or at least I try not to be influenced by them. In fact, my ideal situation is to be cut off from all this when I am in a creative mood. Once I have finished my work, I can come out and debate these issues, but I don't want them to come in between my inspiration and my writing. So, in fact, you should be asking this question to some critics."

Her attitude situates Tadjo in the current generation of African writers in the paradoxical sense that this is the most cosmopolitan of the generations, one that writes without the burden of many of the "isms," including an overly inclusive Africanism and the preoccupation with either a nostalgic or an essential Africa. Indeed, one has the impression that her scholarly work on African-American literature, and likewise her travels beyond Ivory Coast to Europe, the United States, Kenya, and South Africa, are woven together with her native land in her writing. When I asked about the world beyond Africa, especially in relation to her poetry, she told me:

> Yes, my travels have had an impact on my writing in the sense that I am always influenced by my surroundings. I feel enriched by the discovery of a new culture. When writing the beginning of *Le Royaume aveugle,* for example, I was living in Mexico City. I was fascinated by its incredibly rich cultural heritage. I was also there just after the earthquake that took place in 1985, which explains why the novel starts with earth jolts. If *Latérite* was very grounded in the Ivorian soil, *À mi-chemin,* my second collection of poems, bears the influences of my traveling. The center themes are those of exile and alienation.

Although *Latérite* is rooted in Ivory Coast and focuses on connectedness to the land, themes of migration, absence, and loss echo throughout the long recitative. And Tadjo's widely read novel *As the Crow Flies* is haunted by separation, by the gentle abrasion of different cultures, by the grasping for a sense of who one is when one travels across different social classes, continents, or stations of the romantic heart—and by various transients, who appear in the novel as paragraphs detached from everything else:

> We must be living in a squalid century. He begs because he is an albino. Another has drawn his sleeve well back in order to show his stump to effect. He also wears shorts to let people see his rotten leg.

> He is one of those characters you find hanging around on the streets. Not poor enough to get you worried. Neither a hunchback, nor lacking an arm. He is just the sort that you do not even notice. This could have happened in your city or mine.[9]

My question, "What links would you underline in your work to African (or West African) life in general—themes such as the movement toward the cities?" brought an answer that reflects both the rootedness of *Latérite* and the cosmopolitan air of *As the Crow Flies*:

> There are many, many themes. Today in African literature, issues have moved from the classic themes of traditional versus modern life, the city versus the village, whites versus blacks, colonization versus decolonization. First, the diaspora, made of Africans living outside the continent, forms a big chunk of it. Then, with the independences and the disillusionment that followed, African writers look at the dictators in their own countries and the many conflicts that affect their own lives. They also want to talk about everyday life as it happens on the continent—not just disasters or liberation struggles but simply the lives of ordinary people. So, more and more, the themes are those you find in any literature. But African literature for me is about telling the African context, the African view of looking at the world.

Tadjo's style, as much as her themes, constantly awakens curiosity about her goal, even as it rebuffs stereotypes about African tropes and techniques. In *As the Crow Flies,* as with the best prose-poetry, it moves in fits and starts between these two genres. In her prose, as well as in *Latérite,* there is often a combination of abstract and concrete, an aridness and a sense of disorientation and precariousness combining with sky, horizon, weather—an elemental physicality. Distressing change, and the emblematic trees, in the first part of this passage from *As the Crow Flies* remind us of Sony Labou Tansy's *Une vie en arbre et chars . . . bonds*—while the passage as a whole has the power of Rabindranath Tagore:

> We must perform cleansing rites. Make the necessary sacrifices. We must replant our huge trees that have been uprooted, replenish our sacred forests that have been decimated.
>
> Particles of wind were singing and, as at the time of the primal whirlwind, leaves were blown upward into the sky. The word was complete. That word which is at once uttered and silent, both active and inactive. The one possessed only by the initiated.
>
> The gush of wind. Growling from the steel in the heavens. The rain will be dry and hard. There will be nowhere to shelter. You will have to offer your face and uncover your head. The rite will take place in the heart of the city and across the land. Debris will hurtle down the corridors of power.[10]

Latérite is a looping, caressing, chiding mixture of raw elements: fear, adventure, loneliness. It is also a tale of oppositions: personal secrets versus intimate sharing, the sacred arcana of a culture versus private nostalgia, movement, upheaval, and loss versus the search for permanence. The past seeps out of the earth, but the scenes glint with the future. I asked Tadjo about the starkness and about the odd, modern, and unsettling art that makes the physical details—especially the landscapes—spare yet rich at the same time:

What struck me when I discovered the northern part of my country was the fact that the landscape was so incredibly stark. *Latérite* is the name of the red iron earth that you find in the Korhogo area, very much like in some Sahelian countries. It is very hard to cultivate. Then you have this intense heat that seems to freeze everything. Yet in this harsh land there is a cultural wealth that has never ceased to amaze me. The Senoufo people are excellent carvers, reknowned for their art and mud cloth paintings all over the world. Their mythology is complex. They have secret societies and sacred forests. They are highly religious people. I think that in my description of the landscape I tried to show this duality, this contrast.

Several years ago, in a conversation with Stephen Gray, Tadjo commented on the jagged story line of *As the Crow Flies*:

> People say it is like the *nouveau roman,* very discontinuous, or consists of the prose-poems going back to Baudelaire and Max Jacob and all that sort of thing, but also it goes back to oral literature, which always used a *mélange* of genres, freely switching from one mode to the other. That's how I view the work, as coming from that tradition rather than from any European one. . . . I am heavily influenced by the African oral tradition, which has always been very innovative, always looking forward.[11]

Her remarks apply equally to *Latérite,* whose material Tadjo describes as individual poems but whose poems seem to stand in varying degrees of embrace with one another, as if to invite a long and incantatory recitation. Again, then, we find ourselves face to face with the modern moment in African literature and criticism: just when we begin to appreciate the formal sophistication of a new work, its author—while casually pointing to suggestive comparisons of many kinds from outside the continent—directs us to an ancient and unexpectedly dynamic African tradition.

Notes

A Note on Translation

1. See Ngugi wa Thiong'o, *Decolonising the Mind: The Politics of Language in African Literature* (London: James Currey, 1986). See also Simon Gikandi, "Travelling Theory: Ngugi's Return to English," *Research in African Literatures* 31, no. 2 (2000): 194–209, and Phyllis Taoua's recent work, *Forms of Protest: Anti-Colonialism and Avant-Gardes in Africa, the Caribbean, and France* (Oxford: Heinemann, 2002).

2. Réda Bensmaïa, *Experimental Nations: Or, the Invention of the Maghreb* (Princeton: Princeton University Press, 2003), p. 13. Bensmaïa's comment about his readership was made in a lecture delivered in March 1996 in Providence, Rhode Island, as part of an NEH symposium on the literature of displacement.

Epilogue

1. *À vol d'oiseau* was published in 1986, by Éditions Nathan, and in 1992 a new edition appeared from L'Harmattan. It is available in English under the title *As the Crow Flies*, in the fine translation of Wangui wa Goro (Oxford: Heinemann, 2001). The original French edition of *Latérite* was published by Éditions Hatier in 1984.

2. For more on the divisiveness surrounding Negritude, see Peter S. Thompson, "From Negritude to Multiculturalism: A Look Back," *Academic Exchange Quarterly* 3, no. 1 (1999): 72.

3. *Cahier d'un retour au pays natal* has been published in English as *Notebook of a Return to the Native Land*, in the translation of Clayton Eshleman and Annette Smith (Middletown, Conn.: Wesleyan University Press, 2001).

4. Abiola Irele, *The African Experience in Literature and Ideology* (Bloomington: Indiana University Press, 1990), p. 110.

5. Ibid., p. 112.

6. Wole Soyinka, *Myth, Literature and the African World* (Cambridge: Cambridge University Press, 1976), p. viii.

7. Noureini Tidjani-Serpos, *Aspects de la critique africaine* (Paris: Silex, 1987), p. 99.

8. For a more detailed discussion, see Peter S. Thompson, "Negritude and a New Africa: An Update," *Research in African Literatures* 33, no. 4 (2002): 143–53.

9. *As the Crow Flies,* pp. 21, 60.

10. Ibid., p. 76.

11. Stephen Gray, "Véronique Tadjo Speaks with Stephen Gray," *Research in African Literatures* 34, no. 3 (2003): 145.

About the Author

Véronique Tadjo—writer, poet, painter—was born in Paris and raised in Ivory Coast, and has traveled extensively throughout West Africa, the United States, Europe, and Latin America. She holds a BA in English from the University of Abidjan, where she taught for a number of years, and a doctorate from the Sorbonne in African American literature and civilization. When *Latérite*, her first work of poetry, appeared in French in 1984, it was awarded the annual literary prize bestowed by l'Agence de Coopération Culturelle et Technique, a division of La Francophonie. In 2005, Tadjo was the honored recipient of the prestigious Grand Prix Littéraire d'Afrique Noire, presented each year by ADELF (Association des Écrivains de Langues Françaises) to an author from French-speaking Africa for the body of his or her work.

The author of four novels, among them *Le royaume aveugle* (1991) and *À vol d'oiseau* (1992; *As the Crow Flies*, 2001), and a further collection of poetry, *À mi-chemin* (2000), Tadjo is also the editor of *Talking Drums: A Selection of Poems from Africa South of the Sahara* (2000). In addition, she has written and illustrated a number of children's books, including *Le grain de maïs magique* (*The Lucky Grain of Corn*), *Grand-mère Nanan* (*Grandma Nana*), and *Mamy Wata et le monstre* (*Mamy Wata and the Monster*), which was voted one of the hundred most important African works of the twentieth century and for which Tadjo was awarded a Prix

UNICEF in 1993. Her most recent books are *L'ombre d'Imana* (2000; *The Shadow of Imana*, 2002), a volume of reflections on the genocide in Rwanda, and *Reine Pokou: Concerto pour un sacrifice* (2005), an imaginative retelling of the legend of Abraha Pokou, who sacrificed her only son in order to save her people.

A former resident of Paris, Lagos, Mexico City, Nairobi, and London, Véronique Tadjo currently lives with her husband and two children in Johannesburg.

Point de jalousie
Point de rupture
Point de onirique
Point de bonheur
Tu dormais quand je suis entré

×

J'ai senti le bonheur (le désespoir)

Dans la mer tourmentée
J'ai senti
le soleil

Je pense souvent à toi   A ta voix qui résonne
Je songe à ta présence   a tes doigts sur ma peau
Je me souviens d'un moment de jalousie
Je ... sens le bonheur auprès de moi
Quand je te vois ... le point
Je pleure si j'en ai ...
de ... ... si ... nuit
Je rhabille mon coeur
... que le soleil se leva